THE NO-EXPERIENCE-NECESSARY WRITER'S COURSE

"The author is clearly in command of his subject. And his approach is indeed stress-free.

"His tone works well. The reader and potential writer is made to feel that it is possible to write and write well in a variety of places, with a variety of implements, on a variety of schedules, for a variety of audiences.

"He is very qualified, and what he does well here is to share his obvious pleasure in writing and encourage others to try."

—The Gainesville Sun

By the same author

The Writer's Book of Checklists
The Indispensable Writer's Guide
Manuscript Submission
Surviving Freshman Composition
Putting Your Kids Through College
The Truth About College
College: A User's Manual
Future Pastimes (editor)

THE NO-EXPERIENCE-NECESSARY WRITER'S COURSE

A Unique Stress-Free Approach to Writing Fiction and Poetry For Anyone Who Has Ever Wanted to Put Words on Paper

Scott Edelstein

Scarborough House/*Publishers*
Chelsea, MI 48118

Scarborough House
Lanham, MD 20706

FIRST PUBLISHED IN 1990
Fifth printing 1993

Text design by Louis A. Ditizio.
Cover design by Susan Riley.

Library of Congress Cataloging-in-Publication Data

Edelstein, Scott.
    The no-experience-necessary writer's course : a unique stress-free approach for anyone who has ever wanted to write / Scott Edelstein.
        p. cm.
    ISBN 0-8128-8512-0   —ISBN 0-8128-3134-9 (pbk.)
    1. Authorship—Handbooks, manuals, etc. 2. English language—Rhetoric. I. Title.
PN147.E26   1990
808'.02—dc20   90-8019
                                                                      CIP

CONTENTS

INTRODUCTION

Why This Book Is Special

THIS BOOK IS unlike any other book or course on creative writing that you can buy or borrow.

First, this book is for *anyone* who has ever wanted to write. You don't need to have taken any college courses or been to a writer's workshop. You don't have to have read any of the world's great works of literature. You don't even need to have any previous writing experience. *All you need is the desire to write.* If you've wanted to write but never knew how to get started, this book will provide the perfect start.

Second, it's stress-free. You don't have to turn in assignments or live up to anyone else's goals. There are no deadlines, requirements, or pressures of any kind. You can proceed at your own pace, and you don't have to worry whether you're doing any of the exercises "correctly."

Third, it's fun. The chapters are short, lively, and easy and entertaining to read. The twenty-five writing exercises are designed to intrigue you and inspire you to write—not to force you through some stultifying drill. And all the exercises are flexible and open-ended, so you can go anywhere you want to with them.

Fourth, this book will help you discover *for yourself* what it is you have to say as a writer. It will teach you to write what *you* want to write, and it will help you to express it in the manner that best suits your own unique ideas, themes, talents, interests, and temperament. It will teach you to follow your own creative impulses and to trust those impulses. And it will help you to become the very best writer you can be.

This book is inexpensive. You don't have to spend hundreds of dollars on a college class or a correspondence course or a writer's conference or workshop. All you need are this book, a pen, and some paper. Total cost: about $20.

This book is convenient. You can use it when you want and how you want to. You can learn to write without having to disrupt the rest of your day.

But most important, *The No-Experience-Necessary Writer's Course* presents an approach to creative writing that *works*. It's not a book of lofty literary theory that does little more than fill your head with thoughts and clever quotes about writing. It's a practical, down-to-earth guide to writing that centers on the act of writing itself. It will get you writing and keep you writing—not by making demands or assigning tasks, but by helping you discover for yourself the joys and pleasures of putting words on paper.

I know this approach works because I've seen it work, over and over, for hundreds of people who have used it in my creative writing classes over the past ten years. It's an approach that people find inspiring, exciting, and fun. And it's an approach that can work as well for you at home as it does for my students in the classroom.

Although this book has been written primarily for people who have done little or no writing before, it can also be helpful to more experienced writers. If you are already a practicing writer, this book can provide new ideas, inspiration, and energy for your writing. It can help you look at your own writing in new and different ways. It might even open up whole new areas for you to explore in your writing, or it might get your writing going in different and exciting directions.

No one is better qualified than you to put into words what you have to say. This book will show you how to do it, do it well, and enjoy every minute of it—even if you've never tried it before.

Scott Edelstein
Minneapolis, MN

THE
NO-EXPERIENCE-NECESSARY
WRITER'S COURSE

Becoming a Writer in Thirty Seconds

ANYONE WHO WRITES is a writer.

From the time you turn out your first story, poem, or essay—or even your first paragraph, stanza, or scene—you're a writer. It's as simple as that. Anyone who tells you otherwise is off the mark.

Of course, it's unlikely that you'll be able to write great fiction or poetry from the time you first start writing (though this does happen once in a great while). More likely, you'll gradually get more versatile, more creative, and more skilled. As in any other endeavor, the more you write, the better you will get.

But no one should expect you to write great literature from the start. Nor should you expect it yourself.

A lot of other people—mostly other writers with inflated egos—like to make pronouncements like, "You're not a writer until you've written at least three books." Not surprisingly, the person who makes such a statement will have written three or more books. For some reason, there are thousands of people, most of them writers, who feel it is important to define for the rest of the world who is a writer and who isn't. And, almost inevitably, these people include themselves in their definitions of "writer," while excluding almost everyone else.

Forget what these people say. It's nonsense. If it comes

from the mouth of a respected (or even famous) writer, writing teacher, editor, or critic, it's still nonsense.

You may not be a great (or even a good) writer yet. But that's not the point. No matter what you decide to do, you've always got to start at the beginning and then get better and better. So don't put yourself down for being a beginner, and don't let anyone else try to put you down for it. Remind such people that they were once beginners themselves.

Once you've begun writing, you're a writer. Don't worry about your self-image. Don't be concerned with living up to someone else's definition of a writer, because you don't have to do so, now or ever.

If at any point in this book you begin to get worried or scared, reread this chapter. And if anyone looks down his nose at you, give it a tweak and read this chapter again.

The Ten Biggest Fears About Writing—
and How to Get Over Them

HERE ARE THE ten biggest and most common fears in all their negative glory:

1. I can't do it. (Variations: It looks so difficult; I've never done anything like it before; but I'm only a plumber, a doctor, a housewife, an atomic scientist, a receptionist, a mechanic, a janitor, a business executive, a waitress, a tailor, a barber, a social worker, or a big-game hunter. But I never finished grade school; but I've got a physical or emotional handicap.)

2. I don't have any talent. (Variation: Who am I kidding? It's so unrealistic to think that I can write.)

3. I don't have anything (or anything important) to say. (Variations: I don't know what to write about; why would anyone be interested in what I have to say?)

4. I don't know how to say what I want to say. (Variations: But I don't know anything about writing; but I've never taken an English class since high school, and that was years and years ago.)

5. I'll never be as good as the writers I like to read. (Variations: I'm sure other people are much better at writing than I am; the competition is so stiff and there are so many writers out there already, so why bother?)

6. I can get started well enough, but then I get stuck. (Variations: I can never figure out how to end anything; I always lose interest halfway through.)

7. I never know where or how to start. (Variation: I have all these good ideas, but I can never manage to get them down on paper.)

8. What I write might not be any good. (Variations: I might fail, and I can't bear failing; if I can't do it well, or perfectly, from the start, I'd rather not bother with it.)

9. It's so impractical. (Variations: What good will it do me?; if I can't earn money or get a job with it, what's the point?; I could be taking a course in—or reading a book about—real estate, or how to start my own dog grooming business, instead.)

10. I might not enjoy writing. (Variations: It might be painful or hard; what if I hate it?; what if it bores me?; do I *really* want to write?)

There is also an eleventh fear—a general fear of writing. Some people, especially people new to writing, simply tense up or go blank whenever they begin writing something or even think about writing something. This general fear of writing often comes from having had small-minded and sharp-tongued English teachers.

Most beginning writers have at least two or three of these fears, and it's not terribly unusual to have most of them. So if you have these fears, don't worry. In fact, fears of these sorts are normal at the beginning of any new venture.

Nor is it unusual for writers with years of experience to still have their moments of fear or uncertainty. I struggle with fear #8 almost every time I begin a new piece of writing, and when I write fiction I sometimes have trouble with fear #10.

THERE IS ONE tried-and-true way to get over these fears, and it works 99 percent of the time:

Write. Don't spend your time thinking about your writing but never putting words down on paper. Don't busy yourself worrying about the fears. Start writing. If you know exactly what it is you want to write, put this book down right now

20

and get started. If you don't know what to write, keep reading until you reach Exercise #1, then begin writing with that.

The exercises and the remaining chapters in this book will help you gain more and more confidence in yourself as a writer. The more you write and the better you get as a writer, the more you will see how and why most or all of these fears are unfounded and best ignored.

A couple of final words about fear: first, don't wait until all your fears have disappeared before you start to write, because they'll never all go away completely. The trick is to keep writing and trusting yourself *despite* the fears.

Second, don't try to get rid of your fears through logic or argument, because it probably won't work. Most fears cannot be rationalized away or eliminated by confronting them. Instead, admit that you do have some fears and don't let them get in the way too much. Start writing and keep writing, and you'll see that most of your fears will gradually melt away on their own. In the meantime, if you absolutely must go through periods of worry or panic, go ahead and write first; then, when you're done writing, feel free to panic all you like.

The Ten Biggest Myths About Writing

WRITERS AND TEACHERS of writing sometimes have a tendency to make sweeping statements about writers and writing. Most of these are true for the speaker but untrue for most or many other writers. Sometimes they are not even true for the speaker, but they sound good. Here are the most popular of these myths:

1. You must write every day.

2. You must write a certain amount every day, or every time you write.

3. You must commit yourself fully to your writing. (Variations: Writing must be the most important thing in your life; writing requires a 100 percent commitment; you must think and act like a writer twenty-four hours a day.)

4. You must have a room of your own to write in. (Variations: You must have a certain space that you use only for your writing, no matter how big or small that space is; your writing area must be off limits to all other people and creatures.)

5. You must write according to a regular schedule. (Variations: You must write at the same time every day; you must write for a certain amount of time every day.)

6. A writer must be unhappy. (Variations: A writer must be lonely; a writer must be bitter; a writer must be cynical; a writer must be overwhelmed by the unfairness and point-

lessness of existence, or at least act as if he is; a writer must go through periods of despair and/or existential anxiety; a writer must suffer; writing is painful.)

7. You must be completely free from distraction and interruption when you write.

8. You have the responsibility to bare your soul in your writing. (Variation: You should write about the sleaziest, most painful, most personal, and/or most intimate things you can.)

9. A writer needs to be a little bit crazy. (Variations: A writer must be neurotic; a writer must be more than just a little crazy.)

10. Being a writer is a noble and heroic thing.

None of these statements is universally true, nor is any of them even true for most writers. Some of them are true for some writers. Most of them are pure baloney.

Usually statements such as these are little or nothing more than people's ways of rationalizing their own behavior, anxieties, compulsions, or desires. People who think you need to be a little crazy to be a writer are often a little crazy themselves, or at least think they are. People who like to talk about what a noble profession writing is probably feel an undue amount of pride in themselves for putting words on paper.

Some of these statements can actually be harmful to writers. For example, if you have a spouse and a couple of kids, it might be foolish and unethical to put your writing ahead of their needs. If you quit your job and let your family starve because writing is the most important thing in your life, I'd seriously suggest you rethink your priorities.

Some writers do find that they do their best work when they write every day or for a certain amount of time each day or on a regular schedule. Others find it helpful or necessary to be alone in the same private, quiet spot to write. Still others find inspiration only in revealing their own biggest secrets and deepest fears in their writing.

If any of these are true for you, fine. Take them as your

23

personal guidelines and follow them as much as you feel you need to. But also feel free to ignore them whenever you wish. And don't think that they must also be true for all other writers.

As you do more and more writing, you will discover for yourself what your own needs, preferences, and attitudes are. Later chapters will discuss just how to find and follow your own path, and how to determine the times, places, and circumstances for writing that are most helpful to you.

4

The Secret to Writing Well

NO MATTER HOW much you read about weight lifting, it won't do a thing for your muscles. But ten minutes of actual weight lifting a day will build up your muscles within a few weeks. The analogy holds true for writing skills.

The secret to writing well is practice—actual writing experience. In general, the more you write, the better a writer you will become.

Lectures, theories, and the exchange of ideas can be helpful. So can reading the works of other writers. But the single most important learning tool is actual writing. As you write, you will experience personally and directly what all the theories and lectures can at best only point to.

There are limits to all this, of course. There is a point beyond which "more" no longer means "better." If you are writing an hour a day (which is quite a bit, by the way) and progressing very nicely, upping your writing time to ninety minutes a day won't necessarily increase your progress or output 50 percent, or even 10 percent. For some writers the extra time and effort might even result in *less* progress, since they will be pushing themselves too hard. As you write, you'll need to watch your own habits and progress to determine exactly what works best for you.

There are lower limits, too. If you're writing one paragraph a week, you're obviously not going to develop very much or very quickly as a writer. But you might be surprised at how much you can learn, and how much writing you can turn out, writing for ten or fifteen minutes every couple of days.

You should write however much and at whatever pace most naturally suits you. Some people like to write for a few minutes every day. Others might write for a couple of hours at a time, but only twice or three times a month. Whatever your pace or schedule, the more actual writing experience you have, the more you will learn and the better a writer you will become.

Some people naturally write more than others, and some naturally progress faster than others. It's also quite possible for a writer to progress quickly for a while, then slowly (or not at all) for a while, then quickly again.

While it's true that writing poetry is the best way to learn to write poetry, to some degree *all* writing, no matter what its form, will be helpful to you. If you're new to writing fiction but have written a great many things for your job or papers for college classes or thoughtful and intelligent letters, these items will probably help you more with your fiction writing than you realize.

There's no standard answer to the question, "How long do I have to write before I become a good writer?" For some people it may take months; for others, years. Some people write well virtually from the start. But no matter how long you have been writing, and no matter how good you get to be, there is always room for you to grow further as a writer.

5

Getting Started

THIS BOOK CONTAINS twenty-five writing exercises that alternate with groups of chapters. There are also about twenty additional writing exercises at the end of the book. Most of these exercises are my own invention, though some have been borrowed from other writing teachers. Each of them is designed to provide a starting point for your writing from which you can take off in any direction you please.

Although it is possible to use most of the exercises in this book in many different ways, here are the two methods that have worked best for many writers in the past:

THE FORTY-MINUTE START

When you begin an exercise, make an agreement with yourself that you will have exactly forty minutes to write. Note your starting time; as you write, keep track of how much time remains.

Spend the first few minutes contemplating the exercise until you come up with an idea or image from which you can begin writing. If it takes longer than a few minutes to get started, fine; but keep the forty-minute time limit in mind.

Once you have begun writing, keep writing (if you can) for the full forty minutes, or until you come to a natural stopping place or complete the piece.

When the forty minutes are up, stop and look over what you've done. Note down ideas you have for where the piece will go next. Also note down any images, lines, or ideas that might be used later on in the piece. If you prefer not to keep going, fine. Make a mental note of your writing accomplishments over the past forty minutes, and come back and do further work on the piece later.

If, when the forty minutes are up, you find the words and ideas flowing very easily and smoothly, don't stop. Keep going until you naturally slow down, until you come to a good stopping point, or until you have had enough of writing for a while. Then proceed with the instructions in the paragraph above.

The forty-minute time limit is of course somewhat arbitrary. Feel free to shorten or lengthen the period of time to best suit your own work habits and needs.

This method works well for writers who work best with a deadline, who have a limited amount of time available for writing, or who feel lost without some goal or structure.

THE SLOW-BREWING METHOD

Read over the exercise a few times, then spend a few minutes considering and contemplating it. If these few minutes lead to the beginning of a piece of writing, go ahead and write. If they don't, spend a few more minutes in contemplation. If you still haven't come up with anything, move on to some other (non-writing) activity.

Over the next few days, return to the exercise at least once or twice a day, spending a few minutes considering it each time. Continue with this process until something clicks and you begin writing. Then write for as long as you wish.

Try to keep pen and paper with you or near you at all times. You may find ideas or images coming to you at odd or unexpected moments. For example, while bathing you may remember the smell of the attic where you used to play as a child; or you may suddenly imagine the funeral of a famous circus clown while you are riding the bus to work.

If at all possible, start writing as soon as the inspiration hits you, no matter when or where it happens. If this is not possible, try to jot down some notes to refer back to later, when you do have the time and freedom to write. If you don't at least make notes, you may not be able to remember later just what it was that inspired or intrigued you.

This method works best for writers who have a fair amount of time available to write, who are contemplative by nature, or who work best when given as much freedom as possible.

It is perfectly fine to modify either of these approaches, to combine the two methods, to use one method for some exercises and the other for other exercises, or to devise and use methods of your own.

SOME THINGS TO keep in mind while doing the exercises in this book:

None of the exercises is required. If an exercise fails to interest or intrigue you, or if you simply draw a blank with it, skip it and try another one.

You don't have to do the exercises in the order in which they appear. The exercises and chapters have been arranged in a sequence that will be appropriate and helpful for most writers. But if you are inclined to ignore that sequence, feel free to do so.

If at any time you want to modify any exercise, go ahead. The exercises are meant to inspire you and get you writing, to get you to make mental and emotional connections that lead to scenes, images, stories, and poems. *They are not assignments to be fulfilled.*

If, as you are writing, you realize that what you are writing no longer relates to the exercise, *do not* try to force it to fit the exercise. Instead, let the piece go wherever it naturally seems to be going.

Once you've come up with an image or idea that gets you started, begin writing. You don't have to know where the piece is going or how it is going to finish up. Often a piece of writing will create itself, revealing itself to you one step at a time as you write.

You are not limited in any exercise to writing about 1980s America. You can write a piece that takes place in Philadelphia during the American Revolution, on a space station during the year 2140, or in Atlantis during the Later Golden Age.

Your response to any exercise may be fiction, poetry, drama, an essay, or even some new form of writing entirely (except where the exercise indicates that you should write prose). Allow your writing to take whatever form or forms it naturally wants to take. You may well find yourself writing poetry sometimes, prose at other times. You may even write a piece that is, say, part poetry and part fiction.

If an exercise gives you enough ideas, images, or impulses for more than one piece of writing, feel free to write them both (or three or four).

If you get stuck, or if you begin to get weary, antsy, or uninterested, continue to work for another five or ten minutes. If, after this time, you're still stuck, or you still feel uncomfortable, feel free to stop. Don't try to force yourself through the piece. Come back to it later.

Don't be afraid to make your circumstances for writing as comfortable or pleasant as you like. If you work best while sitting under a tree and listening to Pat Benatar (or Pat Robertson), by all means go ahead.

But if you find you do your best writing when you sit in a straight-backed chair with nothing to look at but your notebook, don't be afraid to go that route, either.

It is equally acceptable to write with a pencil, a pen, a typewriter, or a computer.

Don't worry about making errors in grammar, punctuation, spelling, or diction. Just keep writing. You can correct any errors later, when you rewrite. The same advice applies if you are having trouble coming up with the right word, phrase, image, line, or sentence. Just skip it, continue writing, and return to it later. Leave a blank in the spot that needs attention, if you like. By continuing to write instead of toying with one word or line, you will keep the flow of words and ideas coming.

Don't expect things to click with every exercise. Not everything you begin to write will turn out well. People who have used these exercises in the past have found that about half the time they write something they are pleased with—and about half the time they either don't like what they have written, lose interest in the piece, or never get off the ground.

Don't let this rate of failure bother or depress you. Most writers, including some of the best, permanently file away a great deal of material. It is not unusual for a good writer to complete, and be happy with, less than a third of the writing projects he or she begins.

THESE FIRST FIVE chapters have provided you with all the basic background you need. Now it's time to begin writing. Get out some paper, and a pen, pencil, typewriter, or computer keyboard, and turn the page.

EXERCISE #1

IMAGINE THAT YOU are downtown in a major city during rush hour. Suddenly a woman walks toward you, holding a bag. She meets your eyes, smiles, hands you the bag, and says, "Here you go." Before you can say or do anything, she turns and walks off.

Write a piece that begins with or otherwise includes this scene.

THINGS TO KEEP in mind:
- There may not be a human baby, living or dead, in the bag.
- "You" can refer to yourself, to someone else you know, or to a character of your own creation.
- The city can be any real or imaginary one. It can also, of course, go unnamed.
- The piece does not have to end or climax by revealing the contents of the bag. You don't have to reveal its contents at all. In fact, what is in the bag may or may not be important.
- Remember, you can modify this exercise (and all the other exercises in this book) as you choose.

Why Would Anyone Want to Read What I Write?

THIS IS A question that writers, especially beginning writers, ask themselves often—and it's a good question. Experienced writers often ask themselves the same question in moments of doubt or crisis.

The answer to this question is simple and straightforward: people will want to read what you write because it is entertaining, interesting, intriguing, funny, and/or moving. This is the same reason people read stories, poems, essays, and novels by *anyone*. The exact same qualities that make other writers' (including famous writers') work worth reading are the qualities that will make your own worth reading.

Naturally, if your work *isn't* entertaining, interesting, intriguing, funny, and/or moving, people probably *won't* want to read it. But this has nothing to do with what kind of a person you are or what your background is. It's simply that your writing isn't good enough yet. You need to write more and develop your talents further.

Fortunately, if what you're writing now isn't very good, you'll have plenty of opportunity to improve. One of the best things about writing is that no one has to see what you've written until you're ready to show it. It's not like a piano recital, where every mistake you make is immediately heard by everyone in the audience. If a story or poem you're working on has problems, you can fix those problems whenever you like—and no one has to see that piece of writing until those problems are corrected (unless of course you want people to).

As a beginning writer, you may have some trouble determining what kind of work a piece still needs, how much it needs, or when the piece is finished. I'll be discussing these questions in detail in chapter 77. But in the meantime, simply keep in mind that as you gain more experience as a writer, you'll get better and better at making judgments for yourself.

The Fine Arts of Watching and Listening

ONE OF THE most useful skills anyone can have—as a writer and as a human being—is the ability to notice things. It's a skill few people have, though anyone can learn it with attention and practice.

Most of us notice only a few important details in any setting or situation. Usually the details we do notice are those most pertinent or important to us at that moment. Meanwhile, much of the beauty and splendor of the world passes us by.

Put this book in your lap. As you read the next paragraph, keep your gaze focused on this page. Don't look up or around.

What does the ceiling overhead look like? What details do you remember about it? What are its color and texture? Is it perfectly flat, or is it sagging in spots? Are there any cracks or holes? Where? What kind of lighting, if any, is there on the ceiling? What style of lighting is it? How many lights are there? What other details do you remember about the ceiling?

If you're outdoors, try to recall details about the horizon directly in front of you. What shapes, colors, and textures make up that horizon?

Now look up, at either the ceiling or the horizon. How accurate was your recollection? What were you wrong about? What important details did you leave out?

The point of this brief exercise is not to show you how

inattentive you normally are but, rather, to get you to look more carefully at things you see every day but ordinarily pay little attention to.

Why pay such close attention to things as mundane as ceilings and horizons? Because much of the time they're not mundane at all. In fact, many of us miss some of the most beautiful and fascinating things simply because we're not paying attention. This applies not just to our sense of sight but to all our senses.

Next time you enter a room or a store or a theater or someone else's home, deliberately pay attention to the details. How does the light reflect off the mirror? What does the mortar look like in between the bricks above the fireplace? What are the colors and the pattern of the wallpaper?

Then take this a step further. You can not only be open to all the details of a particular setting or situation but also actively seek them out. Try it right now. What does this book smell like? Remove the dust jacket and feel along the spine. What does this feel like? Look closely at the back of your own hand. Notice the veins and arteries running through it. What pattern do they form? Run your fingertips lightly along the largest vein. What do you feel?

This kind of close observation can be done anytime, anywhere—indoors or outdoors, day or night. All five senses can participate. For example, try tasting a food you've never eaten before—or try tasting something that isn't food at all, such as a metal ruler. Put your ear up to an electric clock. What does it sound like? Try smelling a piece of velvet cloth, or running your palm around a bunch of grapes. Don't be afraid to try something strange or unusual.

Paying attention to details also applies to situations and events. When you're watching something happening—or when something is happening to you—try watching very carefully. How are people acting? What gestures are they making? How do their voices sound and what inflections do

36

they have? What do these gestures and inflections tell you? If you like, try eavesdropping on other people's conversations.

Naturally, everything in this chapter has a reasonable limit. *Don't* do anything that might cause harm to yourself or someone else, or that could risk your health, freedom, or reputation.

Why do all this? Two reasons—one practical and one aesthetic. As a writer, one of the best ways to gather insights, observations, images, and things to write about is to simply pay attention with all your senses. And as a human being, using all your senses fully will make your life more interesting, more rewarding, and more fun—because you'll be soaking up more of what the world has to offer.

Anyone can learn to pay more careful attention to details, and to the world in general; but it does take some practice. At first you may want to assign yourself the task of observing one new place or object closely each day, preferably with more than one of your senses. Or, simply tell yourself to find two or three details each day that you never noticed before. Or deliberately spend, say, ten minutes a day keeping your senses as wide open as possible. Eventually keeping your senses alert and open will come naturally, without any effort or thought. At this point, your writing—and very possibly your life in general—may begin to really come alive.

8

Finding Your Ideal Places, Times, and Circumstances for Writing

HOW, WHERE, AND when you write can have a strong effect on your output, your creativity, and your attitude toward writing. The proper circumstances can help your writing flow freely and smoothly. Adverse circumstances might impede that flow and perhaps even cause your creative abilities to temporarily dry up.

These items affect not only your writing, they affect you as a person. An uncomfortable chair, for example, can make you grumpy, or improper lighting can lead to eyestrain or a headache.

Since each one of us is unique, there are no across-the-board rules for the ideal writing situation. Writers vary widely in what makes them productive and/or comfortable. Mark Twain liked to write while lying in bed. Thomas Wolfe wrote standing up, using the top of a refrigerator as a writing desk. Samuel Butler had a special book with which he propped up his writing board at the exact angle he desired.

One of your first tasks as a writer, then, is to discover for yourself under what circumstances you write best and/or are most comfortable. Here are some things to consider:

• Do you prefer a pencil, a pen, a typewriter, or a computer terminal? The particular style, color, or brand of any of these may also make a difference to you.

- Is there a style, size, or color of paper that you prefer? (For some writers this is very important.)
- Do you prefer to work in the same space, or do you like being mobile? For example, some writers enjoy writing in the park, in restaurants, or on the subway; many carry portable writing boards for this purpose. Others, like me, prefer to write in the same spot all the time.
- If you do write in the same spot, how shall it be arranged? How high should the writing surface be? How much empty space nearby is necessary? What tools (pens, rulers, magic markers, paper clips, and so forth) need to be nearby?
- What sort of lighting do you prefer or need? Natural light? Fluorescent light? Light over your shoulder?
- Do you need absolute quiet and freedom from interruption? Will background noise bother you? Will music help or hurt? Should you disconnect the phone while you write? Does noise or activity actually *help* your writing?
- What kind of a view do you want? A brick wall? A window overlooking your garden? A poster of Snoopy? Photos of your kids?
- How much privacy do you need? Virginia Woolf needed a room that was all hers for her writing. Some writers treat their writing areas as private sanctums, which no one else may enter. Others have no trouble writing on the kitchen table while the phone rings, the TV blares away, and four kids have a fight in the corner.
- How much space do you need? A corner? A whole room? A studio separate from your home?
- Do you work best writing whenever the spirit moves you, or do you want (or need) a schedule?
- If you do make a writing schedule for yourself, how long should you write at each stretch? How often should you write? Once a day? Once a week?
- At what times during the day or night do you work best? Soon after waking up? Late at night? Just after lunch?

• What else can you do to support your own writing efforts and/or to make your writing as pleasant and comfortable as possible? Some things other writers have done include putting up attractive posters; keeping a parrot in the same room; keeping a pot of coffee brewing; drinking iced tea (or cold beer, or cola) while writing; bouncing a ball (or throwing darts, or blowing soap bubbles) while thinking; burning incense; and munching on popcorn. Make a list of the things you might like.

You probably know the answers to some of these questions already. The other answers can be determined with some experimentation. Whatever works best for you is what you should do.

Keep in mind that your ideal places, times, and circumstances for writing may change from piece to piece, season to season, or even day to day.

9

Why Do People Write, and Which Reasons are Good Ones?

HERE ARE SOME of the many reasons why people write:

To express their feelings, thoughts, and/or ideas to others.

To grow intellectually, emotionally, psychologically, and/or spiritually.

To get more deeply in touch with themselves.

To explain certain thoughts, feelings, beliefs, or ideas to others.

To convince others of certain ideas or beliefs.

To play with words, images, ideas, and meaning.

To develop their own writing, thinking, and general communication skills.

As catharsis, to get certain thoughts or emotions out—perhaps even to purge themselves of those feelings or thoughts.

To play out and give life to their fantasies, fears, worries, hopes, goals, daydreams, nightmares, and/or predictions.

To make money.

To evoke certain emotions in their readers.

As therapy, to help keep themselves sane, stable, and/or happy.

To get their names in print, and to gain ego satisfaction therefrom.

To temporarily escape from their own everyday lives, and/or to enable readers to do the same.

To help advance their careers as writers or in some other field.

To pass the time.

For the pleasure of the act of writing itself.

As an experiment, to see whether it pleases them or helps them grow.

To entertain others.

To impress others with their talent, cleverness, or depth of feeling.

To improve their lives.

To create great art.

To leave their marks on the world.

To be able to more easily recall important moments of their own lives. (Diaries and journals are frequently written for this purpose.)

To have something to pass on to their children and grandchildren.

To prove to themselves that they can write and/or write well.

These are the most common reasons why people write. Every one of them is perfectly valid. There are hundreds of others, most of them just as valid.

In practice, most people write for several (if not most) of the reasons listed above. This is of course fine—though any one of these reasons alone would be sufficient. Unknown and famous writers usually share most of the same motivations.

THERE ARE SOME reasons why people write, or want to write, that are *not* valid. Here are the most common ones:

To hurt other people, or to get back at them.

To avoid working or fulfilling other obligations.

To make themselves miserable.

You needn't be the least bit ashamed if you're writing mostly to make money or to get your name in print or to show people what a clever and talented person you are. These may not be the loftiest and most noble of goals, but there's certainly nothing wrong with them. After all, money is nice, and recognition feels good. And it's fine to show off if what you can do is worth showing off. Indeed, to some degree even trying to get your work published is "showing off": you're saying, "Here's what I can do, and I think it's worth publishing so that other people can read and enjoy it."

So stop worrying about whether or not you have a right to be a writer, because you do have that right. Stop being concerned about whether you "should" be writing or not. If you want to write, write; you have nothing to feel guilty about.

Now get writing.

EXERCISE #2

IMAGINE THAT YOU are browsing through an old family album, looking at photographs, clippings, and other memorabilia. Suddenly you spot something that surprises you.

Write a piece that begins with, includes, or takes off from this situation.

THINGS TO KEEP in mind:
- Once again, "you" can refer to yourself, some other real person, or a character of your own creation.
- You are missing the point of the exercise if you simply write something like *Dorothy turned the page and saw, to her surprise and disgust, a flattened Hostess Twinkie. "Oh, dear," Dorothy thought. "How did that get there?" She threw the Twinkie in the garbage, wiped off the page, and kept reading.*
- On the other hand, if you wind up writing (for example) a piece about how much Dorothy's son, Martin, had loved Twinkies as a child, and what Martin had written to her in his last letter before he was declared missing in action in Vietnam, then you will have made good use of the exercise.

10

The Universal vs. the Personal

SOME WRITERS, PARTICULARLY beginning writers, misunderstand what it means to write about universals such as love, hate, death, compassion, loneliness, spiritual aspiration, despair, and ennui. (There are plenty of other universals, of course; these are simply the most popular ones.)

These items are universal because they are experienced by a great number of unique human beings. To express these universals, therefore, you need to show them being experienced by particular people, either real or fictional. One of these people may be yourself.

But if you simply write *about* a universal, as a disembodied concept rather than as the result of particular people's actions and circumstances, chances are that your reader isn't going to be moved or even interested.

You have another option: give your reader a group of sensory impressions (sights, sounds, and so on) that *engender* universal feelings in him. Imagine, for example, geese flying south combined with the sound of fallen leaves crunching underfoot. Can you feel something just from these two images? Isn't it the same thing almost everyone feels in late fall?

Whichever method you choose (and you may use both together), keep in mind that universals are best expressed through particular characters, events, and/or images.

Of course, you don't have to deal with burning universal issues at all. It's very possible to write a good story or poem about buying a car or harvesting corn or sitting out on the porch on a hot summer night. Some of our best and most famous writers have written on exactly these subjects. In fact, when a story or poem is done well, it makes the reader feel that something as mundane as harvesting corn *is* in some way significant or important.

I know of writing teachers who tell their students to avoid universal themes and to concentrate on the smaller, more mundane aspects of life. I disagree with the notion that a new writer *shouldn't* deal with basic or important human issues—but it is very true that they aren't the only things worth writing about.

11

What Do I Write About?

YOU CAN WRITE about anything that interests you. There are no limitations.

You don't even have to understand why you're interested in something. If a person, thing, event, or idea attracts or intrigues you, feel free to use it in your writing. If you are interested in chocolate, vampires, Egypt, and 1958 Chevys, write a poem or story about an Egyptian vampire who owns a chocolate factory and drives a 1958 Chevy.

If something interests you, then chances are good that you'll be able to write something interesting or moving about it (or involving it). Good writing can make *any* subject come alive. The more interested in (or excited about) something you are, the more likely your writing is to interest or move your reader.

On the other hand, if *you're* not interested in what you're writing, or in what you're writing about, the odds are pretty good that your reader won't be, either.

Beginning writers sometimes ask me, "What *should* I write about?" They want to know what themes I consider appropriate or permissible; they want to write about the "right" subjects.

But *any* person, idea, thing, or event that attracts you is a "right" subject. It doesn't matter if other people have written stories or poems about it before. (Actually, just about every possible theme has already been handled by many other writers. But no other writer will have quite the same perspective on it as you—so you needn't worry about covering "old" ground.) The only thing you *shouldn't* write about is something that leaves you cold and uninterested.

What you choose to try to publish, or show to others, may sometimes be a different matter. If you want to write a story about two reporters who uncover evidence of wrongdoing in the Nixon administration, fine. But no editor is going to publish the piece because the subject will be too similar to *All the President's Men.*

Finally, it may sometimes be necessary to do some research. If you want to write about sailing but have never been on a boat in your life, then you'll need to either take a few sailing trips or lessons, or at least do a lot of reading on the subject. But you're perfectly free to write a story or poem about sailing even though you're no sailor yourself.

Self as Subject, Others as Subjects

SOME WRITERS LIKE to write primarily or entirely about their own lives. Others prefer to write about other people—real, fictional, or both. Still others (many science fiction writers, for example) write about entirely different cultures or ways of life. And some writers—myself, for example—write material in all three of these categories.

Which is best? Is it a good idea to start out writing about yourself, then branch out to other people? Or is it egotistical to always be writing about yourself?

In truth, any of the three options above—or any combination thereof—is fine, so long as you're writing what you want to write. Some writers are at their best when they're writing about themselves. Others do their best work when they're writing about other people, real or fictitious.

There are other possibilities, too—for example, creating a character with your name and many of your personality traits who is nevertheless *not* you in certain ways. Edward Abbey has built a career out of writing about "himself"—but the Edward Abbey who appears in his essays isn't exactly the Edward Abbey who writes them. It is perfectly valid to fictionalize a portion of your personality or experience; or to create a character that bears some but not complete resemblance to you; or to put aspects of your own personality or life into fictional characters of your own creation.

Locating Material for Your Writing

WHERE DO WRITERS get their ideas? How do they find things to write about?

To some degree, these questions have already been answered in earlier chapters. Once you realize that anything you're interested in is fair game for your writing, you've got plenty to write about. And once you learn to keep your eyes, ears, and other senses open, good ideas, images, and observations will keep coming to you naturally, without your having to seek them out.

Here are some other ways to generate images and ideas worth writing about:

● Take some time just to think. You can sit quietly or go for a walk or lie in bed. Think about what matters to you, then about how you can best express those concerns and feelings to others. Have pen and paper nearby. Write your ideas and images down. This time to yourself can be very useful. For some writers, including myself, it's essential.

● Take some time to *not* think. Again sit quietly or go for a walk or lie in bed—but let your mind wander or go blank. Then notice where it goes and what images and ideas it generates. Write the best of these down. Chances are good you'll come up with something. I get most of my best ideas this way. (Some writers find that actually doing some form of meditation on a regular basis helps.)

- Do things that are new, different, or unfamiliar, just to see what they're like. The more you do and see, the better your chances are of finding new things to write about.

- Experiment. If you've never written a prose poem, try writing one. Or pick a subject or image at random and start with that; for instance, try writing a poem about oysters, or that has oysters somewhere in it. Or write about the three foods, animals, or people you like (or dislike) the most. Or write about the first thing that comes to your mind. Try different ways of getting started, and see what you come up with.

- Don't be afraid to use your intuition. If your gut tells you to write a poem about two truck drivers named Irv and Francine, give the poem a try.

It's not necessary to wait around for the Muse to strike you. You can do this if you want, but it is very possible to get started, and to write excellent fiction and poetry, without your Muse's help.

14

Should I Keep a Journal?

A WRITER'S JOURNAL—also called a writer's notebook—can be a place to record ideas, images, names, phrases, lines, quotes, and other items that come to you, for use later in your writing. Or you can use a journal like a diary, recording your thoughts, feelings, and experiences, perhaps on a daily basis. Or you can use your journal for both purposes.

Physically, a journal can take almost any convenient form: a spiral notebook, a bound blank book, a loose-leaf binder, a folder full of sheets of paper, index cards, a legal pad—or anything else that you find convenient.

Journal writing is one excellent way to get started as a writer. At the very least, writing in a journal can get you used to writing regularly and putting time and effort into your writing. It's also valuable writing experience.

But what's most useful about keeping a journal is the items that go into it. As you grow as a writer, you'll find yourself coming up with ideas, images, and details worth remembering frequently. If you try to keep all of these in your head, you'll forget most of them. But if you write them in your journal, they'll be there for ready reference whenever you need them.

You have the option of writing regularly in your journal or of using it only when you so desire. Some writers like to set aside a certain amount of time per day or week (in some cases at the same hour) to write in their journals. Others, like me, don't feel this is necessary or helpful.

Do I recommend that all writers, or all new writers, keep a journal? No. But I recommend that you try it for a month or two to see how you take to it. If you like it or feel it's useful, great; if not, there's no need to continue doing it.

Some writers carry their journals with them wherever they go, so that if something useful or important comes to them, they can write it down immediately. (Many of these writers carry notebooks that can fit in their pockets or purses for this purpose.) The drawback of this is that if they lose their journals, they have lost most of their ideas and images.

Other writers keep their journals in their homes or offices, in a safe place, but always carry pen and paper with them; they can then jot down ideas and images as they arise, and when they get home they simply transfer their notes from these slips of paper to their journals. (I strongly recommend that you keep a pen or pencil and either your journal or some paper with you at all times, so that no good ideas, images, or phrases get forgotten.)

Personally, I abandoned a physical journal over a decade ago. Instead, I keep several file folders at home, each for a particular project or group of projects, plus one for miscellaneous items and ideas. I always carry pen and paper with me, and when I see or think of something worth writing down, I do so. When I get home, I simply put the slip of paper into the appropriate folder.

An excellent example of a writer's journal appears in F. Scott Fitzgerald's *The Crack-Up* (New Directions). Another useful resource is Joan Didion's interesting and instructive essay on journals, "On Keeping a Notebook," which appears in her collection *Slouching Towards Bethlehem* (Washington Square Press).

15

Forgetting What You Learned in School

MOST OF WHAT we were taught about writing as children (and as adults) has been helpful. But most of us have also been taught at least a few "rules" about writing, or about the English language, that are absolute nonsense. Here are the most common ones:

Never write in the first person or use the words "I" or "me."

Never start a sentence with "and," "but," "anyway," "however," "therefore," "nevertheless," or "I."

Never use slang or colloquialisms.

Never use foreign words.

Never use italics.

Never use exclamation points.

Never write about yourself.

Never use sentence fragments or incomplete sentences.

Never use curse words in a piece of writing.

Always write an outline before you begin a first draft.

Always know how your piece will end before you begin writing.

Always write your title first.

Put the most important or exciting moment of your piece first, so that you'll grab your readers.

Each one of these proscriptions is useless and absurd—but chances are you're still carrying at least a couple of them with you. You should now feel free to ignore all of them.

EXERCISE #3

WRITE A PIECE that takes place in one of the following locations:

A parked car
A phone booth
A closet
A walk-in refrigerator or freezer

THINGS TO KEEP in mind:
- The piece can take place partly in one of the above locations and partly elsewhere.
- Do not simply write a description of one of these four settings. Most people know quite well what the insides of these things looks like. Something must happen in your piece.
- If you can base your piece on an unusual use of one of these settings, such as a walk-in refrigerator full of Halloween costumes or a car parked atop the Goodyear blimp, then you will likely turn out something good.

16

Where and How Do I Start a Piece of Writing?

YOU CAN START a piece of writing anywhere: with a character, an event, a setting, an image (that is, a sight, sound, smell, taste, or touch), an object, a quote, or an interesting phrase, line, sentence, or idea. You can begin by making an outline, by making notes, or just by starting to write. You don't have to know where you're going or what will happen next, and you don't have to pick the "proper" place to start.

Simply choose the place or method that seems most reasonable or workable, or that feels best, or that comes most easily for that particular piece. This should usually work— but if it doesn't, you can simply try starting somewhere else.

A poem or story doesn't have to be written in the same sequence in which it will be read. You don't have to start at the beginning if you don't want to. For example, if you know how your story will end but not how it will begin, try writing your final scene first.

Keep in mind, too, that a poem or story doesn't have to be *read* sequentially, either. (That is, events don't have to occur chronologically.) For instance, in the middle of a story you might jump six years into the past (in what is called a "flashback") to show what your protagonist was like at that time, or to show a relevant incident.

No one is more in touch with your ideas and emotions, and with what you want to write, than you are. Learning to write well isn't a matter of which rules and techniques to use but of understanding, following, and making best use of your own impulses.

As you write a story or poem, you will get ideas, hunches, guesses, intuitions, and desires for how to begin the piece, how to write it, and/or what to do in it. When you get such an impulse, *follow it*. Don't question it, at least not until you've tried it out. Often the impulse will pay off, no matter how strange or illogical it may have seemed at first.

The worst that can happen is that an impulse *doesn't* pay off and leads you nowhere. If this happens, you can always try again with a different approach to the same line, stanza, scene, piece, or idea.

If a critic or writing teacher tells you to do one thing with a piece of writing, and your impulses tell you to do another, usually you should go with your own impulses first. If your own way works, then you made the right decision. And if your own idea or intuition doesn't lead you anywhere useful, you can then wholeheartedly follow the teacher's or critic's advice.

Trusting yourself and following your own impulses will sometimes lead to failure—but that's okay. *Most* of the time it will be beneficial. In any event, the alternative would be to simply do what other people tell you to do. This will never teach you to write well; it will merely teach you to be obedient. In fact, the mature writer knows when to take the advice of others and when to ignore it and proceed however he or she thinks is best.

The more you write, the better you'll get at both following your own impulses and understanding intuitively how those impulses work for you.

17

Who Am I Writing For?

WHAT YOU WRITE and how you write it are in part determined by who your audience is.

If you're writing only for yourself almost anything goes. As long as you understand and are moved by what you've written, it doesn't matter if the entire piece is written in Chinese, Pig Latin, or secret code.

But if you want your writing to speak to other people, you'll need to take into account what they are willing and able to perceive or accept. If, for example, you want to convince a group of liberals that the death penalty is a fine idea, you shouldn't title your essay "Why You Bleeding Hearts Are Wrong," because your audience will be prejudiced against you from the start. A better title might be "Why I Agree with Jimmy Carter," because Carter, a liberal Democrat, happens to be in favor of the death penalty. Liberals will be likely to give at least passing consideration to an article with this title.

The issue is naturally more subtle in fiction and poetry, but the same general rule applies. If you're writing a poem set in Birmingham, Alabama, for a nationwide audience, you're going to have to explain details that a native of Birmingham would take for granted. If you're writing a story for eight year olds, you should be sure to use language that's more or less on a second-grade reading level. And if you're writing a story about a romance between the Russian ambassador to the U.N. and a member of the U.S. Senate, you're going to have to handle it very carefully to make it believable.

While it's important to take your reader into account as you write, it's just as important to realize that you simply can't please everyone. No matter what you write, and no matter how hard you try, there will inevitably be some people who will hate what you've done, and there will be others who simply won't understand it. This will remain true no matter how well you write and no matter how famous you become.

You will usually get the best results by writing for an imaginary ideal reader—someone who thinks much like you do, is reasonably open to what you are doing, and is willing to give your piece a fair chance. In practice, this means writing what you want to write, but tempering how you write it with the knowledge that it's not only for your own eyes but for the eyes of like-minded people as well.

18

The Censor, the Pessimist, the Nitpicker, and the Obsessive Planner Inside You

EACH OF US has several little voices inside that tell us things like, "Oh, this isn't any good" or "This isn't going to work" or "Who's going to want to read *this*?" Here are some other common worries: "This isn't leading anywhere." "Do I dare try this?" "Will I be able to pull this off?" "This piece is beyond my ability." "People will think I'm a pervert and/or crazy." "I'll never be able to salvage this." "This piece needs more work than it's worth." "Maybe I should just give up on this piece." "I can't keep going (or begin) because I don't know where the piece will lead."

Nearly all writers, including famous and talented ones, hear these voices. I certainly still hear them myself. They usually can't be beaten in arguments, but they can be ignored.

What do you do when you hear one or more of these voices? *Write.* Make your best judgments and keep going. If you've got a hunch, follow it. What, after all, are you really risking (and, at worst, losing) other than some of your time and energy? And you will be learning the craft of writing all the while.

What if you get stuck on a certain word, phrase, line, stanza, or scene? Work on it a little while, but don't let yourself stay stuck for long. If, after a few minutes, you've made no progress, skip ahead to another line, paragraph, or scene, and keep writing. You can then come back to the problem later, at your leisure, when you've completed other parts of your piece. These other sections may even provide the solution to your dilemma.

None of this is to say that you shouldn't be concerned about writing well or about getting your piece in the best possible shape. But you shouldn't be worrying about these things until after (at least) a full first draft. Worrying about a piece while it's in its early stages—or before you even get started—may keep you from ever writing (or at least finishing) anything. Save your concerns about quality, appropriateness, direction, and perfection until you're ready to begin rewriting.

By the way, there's nothing wrong with turning out a terrible first (or second or third or fourth) draft. Many of our best and most famous writers turn out *hideous* early drafts. I turn out awful first drafts all the time. *Let* your writing be terrible in early drafts. You can always rewrite and improve it. But if you don't let yourself write those early drafts, good or bad, you'll have nothing to rewrite and improve.

When the censor, the pessimist, the nitpicker, and/or the obsessive planner in your head start chattering away, give them a courteous nod and go about your business—which is to keep writing.

EXERCISE #4

THINK OF SOME of the incidents, events, and experiences in your past that were painful to you, either physically, emotionally, or both.

Pick one of these incidents that you still recall clearly. Ideally, it should be painful enough to be important or significant to you but not so painful that recalling it troubles you. Some good examples might be the time you broke your arm as a child, or the time you made a fool of yourself at the high school prom, or the time you got stuck on the roof repairing the chimney and had to be rescued by the fire department.

Write up your incident from beginning to end, bringing in whatever background or details are necessary, but leaving out anything that is not strictly pertinent. The event may have taken only ten seconds, or it may have happened over the course of months.

Be as truthful and accurate as possible in reporting what happened. Report what you did, said, heard, and saw, but do *not* report how or what you felt. Don't say, "I'd never felt so humiliated" or "I wished the day would end." Simply go through the incident, step by step, just as it happened to you.

Tell your story in prose—no poetry or drama.

THINGS TO KEEP in mind:
- Tell your story as directly, as simply and as straightfor-

wardly as possible. Don't try to add any extra emotion or atmosphere to it. The actual events and details will speak well for themselves, and they will get across everything you felt without your having to explain what your feelings were.

- Use standard English—no heavy dialect or clever, quirky stylistic variations.

- Avoid any tricks or gimmicks. For example, don't withhold important information until the end to create an artificial surprise ending.

- If you wish, you may write the piece in the third person, with *he* or *she* as the subject instead of *I*. You may even make up a character to take your place if you like, but the story must still be the true account of something painful that happened to you, and your character must do and say what you did and said in that situation.

19

The Pros and Cons of Procrastination and Ritual

PROCRASTINATION, LIKE FEAR, cannot usually be defeated by logical argument. Also like fear, it is something that rarely goes away completely. Most writers procrastinate once in a while. This is perfectly normal. Putting off writing is a problem only when it becomes frequent or habitual.

The best way to deal with a recurring urge to put off writing is to simply sit down and write. Let the procrastinator inside you yammer or even rage. Pay it no mind. Just write. Once the words have been flowing for a few minutes, the yammering or raging will settle down and perhaps even disappear entirely.

Sometimes what appears to be procrastination is really its opposite. Before some writers can begin writing, they have to do things like sharpen pencils, set out a stack of blank paper, dust their desks, water the plants, or do the dishes. Often the purpose of these rituals is not to put off writing, but to ready themselves for writing or rev up their intellectual and creative energies. These rituals can work well, provided they lead directly to actual writing and not to further procrastination.

If you have trouble simply sitting down and getting started, you may want to develop a pre-writing ritual of your own. Almost anything will do—cleaning your desk, brushing your hair, doing sit-ups—whatever helps you gear up for writing. Experiment and see what works best for you.

Pre-writing rituals should be kept short; five minutes is ideal, and fifteen minutes is a reasonable maximum. If you find your pre-writing ritual is getting longer and longer, or if it doesn't lead to writing but to more procrastination, drop the ritual entirely. It has become nothing more than a way to stall.

If you do have trouble getting started, there's something else you should look at: how much you are asking of yourself as a writer. Some writers set unreasonable goals or expectations for themselves, especially when they first start out. Often this is simply from enthusiasm, or because they don't yet know enough about their own ability and limits. If you do find yourself putting off or avoiding writing—or, worse, fearing or dreading it—it may well be that you are pushing yourself too hard, or expecting too many results too soon. Try making your goals or expectations more modest, at least for a while, and see if this makes writing easier or more appealing for you. If necessary, drop *all* goals or expectations for your writing for a while.

20

Writers' Rhythms

SOME OF THE most important things you will learn in your first few months of writing are how fast you write, how much (or how long) you can write in any one session, and when you are beginning to run dry and ought to knock off for the day (or week, or whatever).

Every writer has his or her own natural rhythms. Some writers write every day for an hour, some every two to three days for an hour, some once every three to four weeks for a six-hour stretch, some completely erratically. Hemingway wrote five hundred words a day; I do two to three thousand; I've known writers who do ten thousand or more. The point is not to try to write more or faster than other writers—or more or faster than you wrote before—but to write at *your own* speed, at whatever intervals work best, in whatever amounts suit you.

Rhythms apply not only to the act of writing itself, but to thinking, feeling, and processing information. You may find, for example, that you can write every day for a week or so, but that you then need to stay away from writing for three to four days to catch your breath and to let the ideas, images, and feelings simmer inside you. This on/off rhythm of writing and contemplation is quite common.

It's important that, as you write, you observe your own unique rhythms, then learn to work with them. It's just as important that you don't expect something of yourself that you simply can't do—even if (in fact, *especially if*) another writer can do it easily. Quantity and speed are not virtues; talent and artistic achievement, however, are.

21

Writing What You Know and Faking What You Don't

SOME WRITING TEACHERS tell their students, "Write what you know." The other side of this, which is either implied or expressly stated, is, "Don't write about anything you *don't* know much about."

Neither statement is terribly helpful or accurate. Both are true only on the shallowest and most obvious level: you shouldn't write a poem or story about, say, growing up in sixteenth-century India if you know nothing about that country during that era.

But supposing you did want to write a poem on just that topic. You could certainly read a number of books on sixteenth-century Indian history, culture, geography, religion, and philosophy. You'd probably need to do a good deal of research before you could write a poem that accurately captured the flavor of that time—but you could do it.

Actually, to *some* degree you can fudge. Small and insignificant details can be, and often are, wholly imaginary. So long as what you write *feels* right, your story or poem will be convincing—even if the picture you portray isn't 100 percent historically accurate. Will it really matter to your readers whether kings' robes were made of linen rather than cotton? Probably not. (It *will* matter, however, if you have people in your poem spending shekels instead of rupees; most educated readers will catch this error.)

69

Indeed, "write what you know" can be one of the most limiting bits of pseudo-wisdom that a writer can receive. For if each of us *really* could only write about the kind of life he or she had lived, then nobody would be able (or allowed) to write about a foreign culture, or about any culture that existed in the past. Most science fiction would also be "impossible," or unpermissible.

There is another, more useful, way to look at the maxim "write what you know." Regardless of what culture or background any of us come from, all of us share the same human emotions. It is these emotions that all of us writers seek to express, and to engender in others, in our writing. Those emotions that you know well from experience, and that you want to evoke in others, are what your writing, at base, will be "about." The ability to communicate and evoke these emotions is the ability to write creatively. This is true no matter what people, places, events, or images you use in your writing.

22

The Importance of Failure to Good Writing

AS AN INFANT, the first time you tried to take a step you fell down. When you first tried to ride a bicycle a few years later, you toppled over. And a few years after that, when you first tried to make a grilled cheese sandwich, you probably burned it.

Learning any new activity entails the risk of failure. In fact, it entails some actual failure. You can (and should) *expect* some failure in the early stages of anything new.

Writing is no exception. It won't always go easily, and a piece won't always turn out the way you had hoped. This sometimes makes new writers wonder if they should continue writing, or if they have what it takes to actually become good at writing prose and/or poetry.

The underlying assumptions here are that writing always comes easily for talented writers, and that a good writer never writes anything awful. Both of these assumptions are quite untrue.

Talented, experienced writers fail all the time. For every good story or poem that a writer turns out, he or she has likely written another one that's not good enough to show to other people—or that he or she wasn't able to finish at all.

In fact, every first draft that doesn't turn out perfectly is a "failure" in a sense. After all, if it were successful as is, it wouldn't be necessary to rewrite it, would it?

Even if you've been writing twenty or thirty years, each new piece of writing is, in a sense, a new activity to be learned. Certainly writing experience will make the project go easier; but it won't make a perfect final version spring full-blown onto the page. (Actually, this does happen once in a while, even for beginning writers—but don't expect it to happen regularly.)

In writing, failure isn't really a problem. But your attitude *toward* failure can be. If you expect (or want) everything you write to turn out just right, you are destined to be disappointed. In fact, with most of what you write, you must allow yourself to fail before you can succeed. Unless you let yourself write a first draft, even a flawed one, you're not going to complete the draft and go on to draft #2. Let yourself write, even poorly, just to get the words out onto the page. Remember, no one else will see those words until and unless you want them to. You always have the option to rewrite.

You learned to walk, to ride a bicycle, and to make grilled cheese sandwiches in just this way—by failing at first and then eventually succeeding. Writing is no different. In writing, as in most other endeavors, failure is often the first (and most important) step to success. Trial and error are natural parts of the writing process.

But what if a particular piece *doesn't* work out, no matter how long and hard you struggle with it? Put it aside and go to work on another writing project. You can always come back to that unfinished piece later—or, if you prefer, you can forget about it forever.

EXERCISE #5

WRITE A PIECE in which someone or something goes too far.

THINGS TO KEEP in mind:
- "Going too far" can be taken literally, in terms of distance, or symbolically, in terms of overstepping social, legal, or moral boundaries.
- "Someone" can refer to more than one person.

23

The Uses and Limits of Catharsis

THE SINGLE MOST important part of writing is getting words (if necessary, *any* words) onto paper. However, this is not all there is to writing—not by a long shot.

Writing can be extremely valuable as an act of catharsis— that is, as a means of expressing yourself, of getting your thoughts, feelings, impressions, and ideas out. This has obvious emotional and psychological benefits, and thus catharsis is a legitimate reason to write.

However, catharsis is not (usually) equivalent to art. Art usually requires the processing, shaping, and presentation of thoughts and feelings in such a way that they affect readers.

If you're writing only for yourself, then no rewriting of your material may be necessary. But if you want to speak to others, then catharsis becomes only a first step. The rest of this book will teach you the others.

24

Letting Your Writing Find Its Own Way

A STORY OR poem is in many ways a living, breathing entity. As such it has a life of its own—and sometimes a direction or destiny of its own. This direction or destiny may differ from your own hopes or plans for the piece.

Some day you may be writing a poem or story and suddenly realize that it is not going in the direction you had planned or wanted. Perhaps you had intended to use images of gloom and darkness, but instead you are coming up with images of growth and blossoming. Or perhaps you want to make a character clever and manipulative, but instead she is turning out to be vulnerable and naive. Or maybe your three-line stanzas keep expanding to four.

If you notice that what you are writing seems naturally to be going in a direction other than the one you had intended, do *not* try to force it back into line. Instead, let the piece go where it seems to want to go. Strange as it may sound, the piece itself may "know" better than you what is best for it.

It may be that the piece has "grown out" of your earlier plans and expectations. Or it may be that your original intentions were flawed from the start. Or it may well be that the piece has an internal logic that is directing it—a logic that you yourself don't even consciously see or understand yet. But whatever the reason, don't try to force the piece back into line—not at first, anyway. Instead, keep writing in whatever new direction the piece has taken.

It's not necessary to understand *why* a story or poem takes a new direction; in fact, trying to understand may only get in the way, at least during the initial writing stage. Don't worry that you're in uncharted territory. Just keep writing and see what happens.

When you come to a natural stopping place, look back over what you've done. Is the piece developing well? If so, stick with it and with its new direction. Don't try to force it back into its original mold, even if it has departed radically from your original plans.

If you like, you may at this stage try to analyze how the piece is working, where it will go next, or why the change in direction is appropriate. But this isn't necessary, or always helpful.

What if, when the piece is done, it doesn't do what you had originally wanted it to do? That's fine. What's most important is that the story or poem is a good one, that it stands on its own as a legitimate artistic achievement. And if you like, you can now begin a new piece that does what you had originally wanted your earlier piece to do.

What if you follow your piece's natural direction and it leads nowhere, or to a dead end, or in circles? Simply go back to where the piece started going astray and *now* try to squeeze it back into your original mold. If it still resists, consider alternate directions the piece might go in. Use the exercises in this book, particularly Exercise #8 (page 108), to help generate images and ideas.

The Mysteries of Creativity

SOMETIMES WHEN YOU write, the words will seem to pop mysteriously into your head (or onto the page) without your willing them. Other times you may know exactly what to write next without knowing where the ideas are coming from. Or you'll know that a particular word, phrase, image, or line is right, without knowing why.

All of this may seem surprising as it happens—or it may feel perfectly normal.

The fact is that many writers don't understand how they do what they do—they just do it. Some write stories, poems, and other pieces without knowing what those pieces mean—but somehow knowing that they are "right."

It's not necessary to know what you want to say to write a piece. Nor is it necessary to understand how your piece is working—even while you're writing it. Just keep writing, following your creative impulses, and making your best judgments.

When you reread your work, you may find that there are things in it that you hadn't consciously intended to add but that work well nevertheless. Symbols, metaphors, puns, and double and triple meanings often make their way into stories and poems in just this manner.

A Short Course in Temporary Insanity

BY THE TIME we get to high school, most of us know what makes sense and what doesn't. In fact, by the time we get to high school, most of us have developed very rigid ideas about what is logical, what is acceptable, and even what is real. These ideas enable us to communicate with one another, keep us from getting too confused, and help us to make it through the day.

Language is one of the main tools we use to reinforce these rigid ideas. But just as words can reinforce what we think, believe, and agree on, they can show us new and unusual ways of looking at things.

A good example of this is the "huddled, pinned lights of towns" from John Edward Sorrell's poem "Shelter" (pages 281-82). We don't normally think of lights in this way. Taken out of context, the image seems strange, perhaps even a bit crazy; lights, after all, can neither huddle nor be pinned. But when we realize that the person seeing these lights is flying above in an airplane, preparing to drop a bomb, then suddenly the image makes sense to us and moves us.

This is how metaphors, similes, and symbols (see chapter 29 for definitions) work. They enable us to see, sense, or understand something in a way we normally wouldn't—and often in a way that doesn't fit in with our everyday ideas and beliefs.

Actually, we sometimes do just this sort of thing in our normal conversations. If I look out the window and say "It's raining buckets," you understand immediately that rain is coming down very hard; you don't assume that thousands of buckets are tumbling down from the sky.

You can use alternate logic—the logic of imagery, metaphor, simile, symbol, satire, and intuition—in your own writing. In fact, as you write, you'll find some of these appearing quite naturally, without your trying to deliberately think them up. Don't suppress or reject them. Let them come. Sometimes it is this alternate logic, or even outright non-logic, that makes a story or poem work.

If you get an "illogical" idea or image and it seems to fit, use it. You don't have to be able to explain it to anyone; indeed, you don't even have to understand how or why it works yourself.

This doesn't mean that a story or poem based on nothing but "normal" logic can't be good. Indeed, much of our best literature is entirely logical from beginning to end.

The point here is simply not to be afraid to be logical, alternately logical, or thoroughly illogical. Be willing to do whatever works, no matter how or why it works, and no matter how weird—or normal—it may be.

EXERCISE #6

WRITE A PIECE about hoopies or zazen, or one in which either hoopies or zazen appear. You must of course decide what you want hoopies or zazen to be.

THINGS TO KEEP in mind:
- *Hoopies* and *zazen* are in fact real words currently used in the English language, though they are not likely to be found in most dictionaries. However, the point is not to try to guess what they are, but to use your imagination and intuition to create your own zazen or hoopies and actually use either one in a piece of writing.
- Do not simply define either word and have that definition stand as your piece of writing. You should write a whole piece in which hoopies or zazen—as beings, things, or concepts—actually appear.
- Hoopies or zazen can be either singular or plural. If you make either word plural, it is fine to have an individual hoopy or zaz in your piece.
- Hoopies or zazen can refer to people, animals, plants, man-made items, concepts, states of mind, philosophies—anything at all, real or imaginary.
- If you want to write a piece that uses both hoopies *and* zazen, that's okay. But if doing this starts to create a problem, pick one of the two and stick with it.

If you are one of the few people who actually know the real definition of either or both of these words, you should still make up your own imaginary hoopies or zazen, rather than write about the real things.

The actual definitions of both words appear below. However, do not look them up until after you have written your response to this exercise.

Hoopies were what people in southern and eastern Ohio called the people upriver in West Virginia early in this century. This slang term, which was intended as an insult, referred to the fact that there were many barrel factories along or near the Ohio River, on the West Virginia side. Some Ohioans still use the term as an insulting reference to West Virginians—even though the barrel factories closed down decades ago.

Zazen is a Japanese word meaning "sitting meditation." It is the form of meditation practiced by Zen Buddhists. When Zen came to this country, the word "zazen" came with it, and now it is part of the English language.

27

Do I Have to Finish?

ONCE YOU'VE BEGUN a story, poem, or other piece of writing, you're under no obligation to keep working on it steadily until you're done. In fact, you're under no obligation to finish it at all.

There's no reason in the world why you have to plow through a poem or story from start to finish. If this method works for you, great—use it. But it is possible to write an excellent story or poem in bits and pieces, and even in fits and starts. I know of pieces that have been written over *decades,* a few pages at a time.

If you're having a good deal of trouble with a piece, or if you simply lose interest in it, feel free to put it aside and move on to another writing (or non-writing) project. You can always come back to the first project later—the next day, later that month, or three decades in the future. You also have a perfect right to abandon the project forever, if you so desire. What you should *not* do is feel guilty about quitting in the middle, or, worse, force yourself to finish a piece simply because you started it. That would be obsession, not creativity.

No serious writer expects that every piece he or she begins will work out or be worth completing. Writing frequently results in false starts, pieces that lead nowhere, and ideas that don't pan out. Writers—including talented writers—give up on projects all the time.

In fact, sometimes if a piece isn't working out, it may be because it *can't* work out. Perhaps your basic premise isn't strong enough, or the structure of your piece simply won't support what you're trying to say, or what you're trying to do is too complicated or delicate. When you do get stuck, you should spend some time trying to get your piece unstuck (see chapter 63 for details); but if this doesn't work, sometimes the best thing to do is put the piece aside, at least for a while. (Indeed, sometimes you can get stuck by pushing too hard, by trying to finish a piece before it's ready to be finished. It may be that it needs time to brew inside you further.)

This doesn't mean you should be lazy or that you should give up on a piece if it doesn't come quickly or easily. But it does mean that you always have the right to say, "Enough!"

28

How Important Is Reading to Writing?

SOME WRITERS AND writing teachers insist that you can't write well unless you are widely read. Some claim that you can't be a decent writer unless you've read a particular group of books or writers. And a few insist that you can't begin to write (or at least write well) until you've become familiar with the major works, authors, and/or literary periods of Western civilization.

All of this is nonsense. For every book you "must" read if you are to become a writer, I can show you ten talented and successful writers who have not read that book. As one of my students once said, "Shakespeare never read *Moby Dick,* and his writing turned out pretty well."

Reading (especially within your own genre) helps, and reading widely helps a lot. But it isn't essential to writing. And certainly you don't need to read any *particular* literary works to write well.

Nor is reading an adequate substitute for writing. If you want to learn to write well, then the most valuable activity you can engage in is writing itself.

In fact, some writers (including me) sometimes *avoid* sitting down to write by reading excessively. And I've met beginning writers who were so busy giving themselves the "necessary background" in reading that they got very little actual writing done.

You should feel free to read as much, or as little, as you please—so long as reading doesn't cut substantially into your writing time, in which case you should be writing more and reading less. Reading and writing, while mutually reinforcing, are nevertheless separate activities. One cannot replace the other—though they can inspire each other.

29

Fifty-Seven Terms You've Always Wanted Defined

HERE ARE SOME terms that are commonly used by writers, writing teachers, and books and articles about writing. Please read all the definitions carefully; some of the terms may not mean what you thought they did. You may also discover that some people you know (including writing teachers) or books you've read have misused some of these terms. A few of these terms, in fact, are misused regularly and widely.

Allegory
A story in which the characters, and sometimes the plot and/or setting, represent institutions, objects, and/or ideas. George Orwell's *Animal Farm* is a contemporary allegory.

Ambiguity
Anything that can be taken two or more ways at once. Ambiguity can be either harmful or helpful, depending on its use (or misuse). For example, ambiguity should be avoided when you are seeking clarity and certainty. However, ambiguity can be used positively. Consider this haiku by the Japanese poet Basho:

The cold winter wind:
Something painful swells the cheeks
        of her lovely face.

The "cheeks of her lovely face" can be taken literally as a reference to a woman of Basho's acquaintance; it can also be taken metaphorically, as a description of the environment at wintertime. Both interpretations are valid, and both move the reader. Thus, the ambiguity adds strength to the poem. Something that expresses an ambiguity is said to be AM-BIGUOUS.

Character
Any person who appears in a story, poem, novel, play, or other literary work. A character can also be an animal or imaginary being—for instance, Lassie, the Cowardly Lion, Godzilla, etc.

Characterization
The creation of characters in a literary work.

Cliché
Any word, phrase, idea, or event that has been used so frequently that it has lost its power and freshness. Examples: "It's raining cats and dogs"; "Where's the beef?" An image can also be clichéd—for example, the plump mother wearing an apron. Clichés should be avoided or, when spotted during rewriting, eliminated or replaced.

Climax
The moment of greatest tension in a literary work. Normally a resolution of this tension follows shortly or immediately

thereafter. A literary work can have more than a single climax.

Denouement
The final untangling or resolution of events in a literary work.

Development
The building up of imagery, plot, characterization, and/or ideas.

Dialogue
(Also spelled DIALOG) 1) Any discussion between two or more people or characters. 2) Any talking by one or more characters or people. (A MONOLOGUE—also MONOLOG—is a speech made by a single person or character.)

Diction
The choice of words. Refers to shades of meaning rather than to matters of grammar or punctuation. "I sat down in the chair that was mine" is grammatically correct but has poor diction.

Draft
A version of a piece of writing that has been written more or less from beginning to end. For example, the third draft of a piece is the third complete version.

e.g.
Abbreviation for Latin words meaning "for example." A

comma is usually put after it. Commonly used as a space-and timesaver. Example: "This book covers many writing topics, e.g., getting started, rewriting, and submitting work to editors." Not to be confused with "i.e."

Ellipsis Points
Three points or dots, typed as periods (. . .) and used to indicate a pause, a trailing off, or an omission of words. Use four dots to indicate the omission of the *end* of a sentence or a whole sentence.

Epiphany
A moment of awakening or realization on the part of either a character or the reader himself—or both.

Flashback
Any scene in a literary work that takes the reader out of the standard sequence of time into the past.

Focus
A rather vague term that has been used and misused in a variety of ways. It can refer to the central theme of a piece, to its central character(s), or to its point(s) of view. When some-one uses this term, it is best to ask what it means.

Foreshadowing
Hinting or implying future developments through imagery, dialogue, plot, diction, detail, or other means. For example, if in an early scene of a story we see a woman walking through a cemetery, we are perhaps being subconsciously prepared for her to die or witness a death later in the piece.

Genre

Any general type of writing—e.g., fiction, drama, or poetry. Specific fields of writing such as horror, romance, and science fiction are also called genres.

Grammar

The rules governing the use of language in reading, writing, and speech. Includes the conjugation of verbs, direct and indirect objects, and other functions and relationships of words in a sentence. Grammar involves specific rights and wrongs—as opposed to diction, which can be poor, fair, good, or excellent.

Hyperbole

A deliberate (and often extreme) exaggeration, often in the form of a metaphor or simile, meant to lend emphasis and not meant to be taken literally.

i.e.

Abbreviation for the Latin words meaning "that is." Example: "At that hour, Mr. Murray was usually indisposed—i.e., busy flirting with his boss's secretary." Not to be confused with "e.g."

Image

Any sensory impression or detail, or group of impressions or details, used in a piece of writing. Most often refers to sight, but can also refer to other senses.

Imagery

The use of images.

Irony

1) A figure of speech in which the intended meaning is the opposite of the literal meaning. For example, "Kareem Abdul-Jabbar said to Gary Coleman, 'Hi there, big fellow.'"
2) An outcome or occurrence opposite to the one anticipated or desired. Example: the student who works hard all term flunks his finals while the one who scarcely opened a book passes with high marks. Often misused to mean "strange" "unusual," or "unexpected." Something expressing irony is IRONIC.

Italics

Letters slanted to the right to denote accent, emphasis, or importance. Should not be overused. Also denotes a book, magazine, or play title, or words from a foreign language. *This sentence is in italics.* To indicate italics in a typed or handwritten manuscript, simply underline the appropriate words.

Metaphor

The comparison of one person, thing, or idea with another, either directly or by implication. Normally the items being compared are in most respects quite different, and usually the comparison is not logically or literally true. Example: "Your girlfriend's a real fox." (See also "SIMILE.")

Mood

The general feeling or atmosphere created by a piece of writing, or a portion thereof. Can also refer to the feeling or atmosphere of a particular setting in a literary work. Slightly different in meaning from "tone," but the two are often (improperly) used synonymously.

91

Narration

The relating of a sequence of events or ideas. A NARRATOR is a person or character who narrates; a NARRATIVE is a piece of writing, or portion thereof, that employs narration. It is possible for a literary work to be devoid of narrative, narrators, or both.

Pace or Pacing

The speed at which significant events, or events in general, occur in a literary work. If a great deal happens in a few lines, the pace is rapid; if events take pages and pages to play themselves out, then the pace is slow. Each stanza, line, section, paragraph, or scene in a piece may have its own pace; indeed, most literary works are slow-paced in some sections and fast-paced in others. The term "rate of revelation" is synonymous.

Paradox

Two or more ideas, observations, images, or assertions that on one level contradict one another but on another fit together or make sense. Example: "A writer can make a fortune, but he can't make a living."—James Michener

¶

This symbol simply means "paragraph." It is normally placed between two sentences to indicate a spot where a new paragraph should begin.

Parody

A form of humor in which a person, his ideas, and/or his manner of writing or speaking are imitated and exaggerated to the point of absurdity. Events, institutions, and publications can also be parodied.

Plot

The sequence of significant events in a literary work. Not all literary works have a plot, though most fiction pieces do. A piece may have more than a single plot. A *subplot* is a separate sequence of events, which is of genuine but secondary importance, sometimes (but not necessarily) related to the main plot. A piece of writing may have no subplots, or it may have several.

Poetry

Any literary work in which the basic unit is the line and the basic larger unit the stanza. (See chapters 82-87 for a complete discussion of poetry and poetic terms and devices.)

Point of View or Viewpoint

The character through whose eyes a particular event, image, or scene is viewed. If a character purports to be the narrator of a piece (or section of that piece), then that piece or section is normally (though not always) from that character's viewpoint. A piece can also be from its author's point of view—or from the viewpoint of an imaginary author of your creation.

It is possible to write in the third person but nevertheless have a distinct point of view. Example: "Suzanne saw three small children walking toward her, and she couldn't help wondering if her own children were safe." It is also quite possible and permissible for the point of view to change from one portion of a piece to another.

Finally, it is possible to write a piece (or portion thereof) in what is called the omniscient viewpoint. Such a piece is written in the third person, and the disembodied "narrator" can see into the people's heads, into the future, and into hidden causes and motivations. Kurt Vonnegut's *Breakfast of Champions* is written, in part, from an omniscient point of view.

Prose

Any writing that uses the sentence as its basic unit and the paragraph as its larger unit. Stories, novels, essays, newspaper articles, and personal letters are all forms of prose.

Protagonist

The main character in a literary work. A piece of writing can have more than one protagonist. The movie *The Big Chill,* for example, has several protagonists. The protagonist of a piece may or may not be its narrator. A literary work may also have no protagonist at all.

Rhythm

1) The flow of sound in a literary work, particularly the pattern of accented and unaccented syllables. 2) The deliberate variation of pace in a literary work. Not to be confused with "rhyme."

Satire

A form of humor that involves making fun of a person, thing, event, idea, or institution, usually through exaggerating one or more of his/her/its qualities. Unlike parody, satire does not pretend to *be* the person or event being made fun of.

Scene

Any self-contained section of a literary work that occurs in the same physical space, takes place in the same span of time, involves the same character (or group of characters), and/or is written from the same point of view. Often misused to mean "setting" or "situation." When someone talks about "setting a scene," he or she usually means "establishing the setting" or "establishing the setting and situation."

Setting
Where and when a particular image, scene, or piece of writing takes place.

Simile
The comparison of one person, thing, or idea with another, using the word *like* or *as*. Example: "Alan smokes like a locomotive."

Situation
The past and present circumstances leading up to and governing the events in a particular scene.

Soliloquy
A monologue spoken by a character in a play.

Stanza
A grouping of lines in a poem. Stanzas are separated by blank vertical spaces called STANZA-BREAKS.

Stereotypes
Characters with simplified, one-dimensional personalities. Stereotypes typically have a very limited range of expression, often limited solely to those actions and expressions judged "typical" for the ethnic, professional, or national groups of which they are members. Stereotypes are normally to be avoided, except for very minor characters or satiric purposes.

Stream of Consciousness
A literary technique in which the viewpoint is from within

one character's head. That character's thoughts and feelings thus become the reader's central (or only) mode of perception. Pieces written in stream of consciousness may use standard English (as in Saul Bellow's *Mr. Sammler's Planet*), or they may use a modified English meant to simulate the activity of human consciousness (as in portions of William Faulkner's *The Sound and the Fury*). The term is often improperly used to mean "writing whatever comes to mind in a steady stream." Stream of consciousness is an advanced literary technique requiring much care and precision; writing whatever comes into your head, while valuable in its own way, is something very different.

Style
The particular combination of pacing, diction, syntax, tone, and voice used in a literary work or portion thereof. A writer may have a unique, recognizable style, or he or she may alter his or her style from one piece of writing to another.

Surrealism
An approach to writing (and other arts) in which reality as we know it is bent out of shape for emotional effect. In a surrealist work, images and events are often illogical or impossible on the literal level. In a successful surrealist work, those images and events nevertheless move us or make emotional sense.

Symbol
Any image, object, person, or event that evokes a meaning other than itself. In sophisticated prose and poetry, things, people, and events simultaneously make sense literally *and* symbolically. Symbols can be overt (as in allegory) or subtle, and they can work consciously, subconsciously, or both. (See chapter 44 for more details and an excellent example.)

Symbolism
The use of symbols.

Syntax
The way sentences are structured. Often misused to mean grammar, diction, or both. In my writing classes, 95 percent of all students have heard the word used repeatedly, often in relation to their own writing—but less than 10 percent know what it means. The sentence "I plan to be throwing the ball to you" has poor syntax.

Theme
The central concern or statement of a piece of writing. A theme may be very specific (e.g., the United States needs to build up its armed forces by at least 50 percent), very general (e.g., the history of birdhouses, or life is absurd), or anywhere in between. It need not be explicitly stated in a piece or even fully realized or understood (at least consciously) by the author.

Tone
The way a piece of writing (or a portion thereof) sounds. Similar to but nevertheless not the same as "mood." For example, the tone of a piece can be cheery but the underlying mood creepy, as in *Arsenic and Old Lace*.

Usage
The general category of rules and standards for language. Includes grammar, spelling, punctuation, diction, and syntax.

Verse
Synonymous with "poetry."

Voice
The manner in which a narrator speaks or writes. Includes all the elements of style. Nearly (but not quite) synonymous with "tone."

More definitions appear in chapters 49-50, 54-56, 59-61, 85, and 87.

EXERCISE #7

WRITE A PIECE in which a man or a woman empties a bucket.

THINGS TO KEEP in mind:
- What is in the bucket may or may not be important or significant.
- It is not necessary to make a mystery out of what is in the bucket, though you may do so if you wish.
- There has to be some point, plot, or effect to your piece. Emptying a bucket should not be the only thing that happens in it.
- If you have some difficulty determining whether the person emptying the bucket should be a man or a woman, make that person the same sex you are.
- If you wish, more than one person can empty the bucket, or more than one bucket can be emptied.

30

Can I Work on More Than One Piece at a Time?

THIS IS REALLY two separate questions. The answer to the first—"Is it *permissible* to work on more than one piece of writing at a time?"—is an unequivocal yes. It is fine to work on two, three, or even a dozen different pieces simultaneously, or to work on one for a while, then move on to another (or several others), then back to the first. At any given moment, I am usually working intensively on one project, writing bits and pieces of one or two others, making notes on half a dozen, and thinking about half a dozen more.

It is also just as acceptable to work solely on a single project from start to finish before beginning another.

The answer to the second question—"Is it a *good idea* for me to work on two or more pieces simultaneously?"—differs from one writer to the next. It all depends on your work habits, lifestyle, creative and physical rhythms, patience, and ability to juggle tasks. Some writers find that working on two or more projects at once provides a release valve: when they get tired of (or bored of, or burned out from) working on one piece, they simply move to another. Multiple projects can often reinforce and provide inspiration and energy for one another.

But other writers find that working on two or more projects simultaneously is tiring, distracting, confusing, or upsetting.

You may need to experiment to see what best suits your own cycles and needs. Don't be afraid to try different combinations and variations. Keep in mind that if you are stalled on a particular piece, one of the best things you can do is put it aside and work on some other writing project for a while.

31

Reading Your Work Aloud

GOOD WRITING MOVES readers in two ways: through what it says and means, and through the way it sounds. Even when you are reading something silently, you are mentally sounding out the words and "hearing" them spoken.

The best way to truly hear and feel the rhythms of your own prose and poetry is to read your work aloud. Reading aloud also allows you to get a much stronger feel for how your piece is working, where it is going, and what needs rethinking or rewriting.

I'm not talking about reading your work before an audience; I'm talking about reading it aloud to yourself as a part of the writing, rewriting, and editing process.

Anthony Burgess, the author of *A Clockwork Orange,* insists that "writers write well only when they listen to what they are writing." I read my own work aloud after each draft, after each stage of writing and rewriting, and each time I think a piece (or portion thereof) is finished. And when I get stuck, or when I have a word, phrase, sentence, or paragraph that just won't come right, I stop and read that portion aloud repeatedly. This enables me to understand (or at least intuit) what the problem is. I then try out various ways to fix the problem by reading them aloud. When the passage both sounds and feels right, I know I've gotten it fixed.

When you read your work aloud to yourself, don't hurry or mumble. Read loudly, slowly, and very clearly. The better you read, the better your work will sound.

This is an extremely important part of writing and rewriting; don't overlook or avoid it.

32

Saving Everything You Write

WHENEVER YOU WRITE something creative—whether it be a finished piece, a draft, a single line or paragraph, or even notes on a project yet to be begun—*save it. Never* throw it away. Put it on a shelf, in a file folder or envelope, or even in a shoe box. But don't toss it out.

You never know when something you have written will prove valuable to you, no matter how awful you might think it is now. The failed poem of today may be the seed of an excellent one a month, year, or decade from now. Even a single line, image, or observation may someday provide the burst of inspiration for something excellent—even if today it strikes you as cliched or insipid.

It might even provide inspiration for someone else. When science fiction writer Lisa Tuttle found herself with a story fragment that she simply couldn't finish, she filed it away and hoped that someday she'd be able to do something with it. Years later, fellow SF writer Steven Utley showed her a fragment of his own that he couldn't do anything with. The two unfinished pieces fit together perfectly into a complete story, which was later published in *Fantasy and Science Fiction.*

Saving everything you write means saving it indefinitely, not just for a few weeks or months. I've written successful pieces based on notes and drafts written nearly a decade earlier.

But don't just *save* this material—use it! Once or twice a year (or more often), take out your collection of fragments, notes, drafts, and failed and unfinished pieces and see what raw material you can mine from it. These items are also worth looking through when you are stuck in the middle of a piece and can't figure out where to go with it; sometimes the answer will be in your collection of word-scraps from the past.

If you save something, it is always available. Once you throw it out, though, it is gone forever.

33

What Does It Mean to Be Meaningful?

I'VE OFTEN HEARD people ask about a story or poem, "What does it mean?" This is a legitimate question, but it can't always be easily answered—and sometimes the author can't answer it at all.

Many of us were taught in high school (or elsewhere) that each piece of writing has a specific meaning—a clear-cut statement that the piece can be boiled down to. This could hardly be further from the truth, at least as far as fiction and poetry go. (Essays can sometimes be boiled down, though normally good ones can't be without losing most of their effect.)

Some fiction and poetry does have a specific *message,* e.g., "truth is more important than glory," or "nature is beautiful." But the *meaning* of a literary work goes beyond its mere theme or message. After all, if the only purpose in writing a poem were to tell readers that nature is beautiful, there'd be no reason to write the poem at all. It would be enough to write "nature is beautiful," and leave it at that.

What the author of such a poem wants to do, of course, is not merely deliver a simple message but express the magnificence of certain aspects of the natural world through a particular combination of images and/or events. The reader is not merely told of that beauty, but shown it; as a result, he or she is able to feel that magnificence, rather than merely be aware of its existence.

The meaning of a literary work—even a simple one—goes well beyond a statement of its central premise, theme, or message. Indeed, many successful literary works have no straightforward messages at all.

In short, meaning is not message. (As a great film mogul once said, "When I want to send a message, I call Western Union.") Meaning is emotion. What a piece means is how it makes its readers feel.

When you write, you don't have to communicate a specific message to your readers—though you certainly may if you want to. What you *do* have to do is evoke emotions—fear, anger, exhilaration, joy, despair, laughter, and/or surprise.

EXERCISE #8

EVERYONE HAS CERTAIN sights, sounds, and smells that touch him or her deeply. For me these include the sound of a train whistle in the distance, the ticking of a grandfather clock, the sight and sound of laundry flapping on a line in the wind, the feel of cold winter air on my face, and the sight of huge factories at night, with their blinking lights and billowing smoke.

I don't really know why these things move me, but they do, and so I often use these images in my writing.

THIS EXERCISE CONSISTS of three steps:

First, take about twenty minutes to think of some of the sights, sounds, smells, and tastes that move you. You may keep your eyes either open or closed.

When you touch on an image that moves you, write it down. If you like, you may savor it for a while, to see if it leads to other images.

It's not necessary to understand why a particular image affects you as it does. Simply write it down, then continue your search for other images.

You don't need to be hurried or systematic about this. Be relaxed in your search.

If you come across something that touches you in a negative rather than a positive way, write that down, too.

Keep going until you have a list of ten or more items, or until you can feel yourself running dry.

Next, take another fifteen or twenty minutes to let your mind wander completely freely. Don't consciously continue your search for images and impressions, and don't think about anything in particular; but don't force yourself to empty your mind, either. Let your awareness go wherever it wants to go. Follow that awareness wherever it leads you.

After a bit, or perhaps even immediately, some images and impressions will come to you. Let them come, whatever they might be. Write down the ones that move you in some way.

Again, you may keep your eyes either open or closed. Most people prefer to close their eyes for this part of the exercise.

Don't worry if some of the images surprise you, shock you, or seem to come out of nowhere. Write them down anyway. If something makes little or no sense, write it down if it nevertheless touches you in some way. If an image frightens you, write it down, too—but if it frightens you enough that you want to stop the exercise, by all means stop.

Third, spend a few minutes looking over what you have written down. Then use one or more of your images and imaginings to begin (or as the basis of) a piece of writing.

THINGS TO KEEP in mind:

• Remember, you don't have to be able to explain why any of the things you have come up with move you, nor is it necessarily important that you understand why yourself. What is important is that these things do move you—which means they are likely to move readers as well.

• You do not have to write about yourself. If you like, you may write a piece that centers around characters of your own creation, or that involves no human characters at all.

• The image or impression that gets you writing does not have to be central to what you write. It may appear in your piece only for a moment—or even not at all.

● The human mind is constantly generating all kinds of images, some of them at random. If, abruptly and for no reason, you come up with, say, an image of striking someone with an ax—or something equally gruesome or unsettling— it does not mean there is anything wrong with you, and it is almost certainly nothing to worry about.

34

The Proper Use of Salt

SOME PEOPLE ARE wiser or more knowledgeable than others. Some have experience or expertise in a particular field. Some have very good judgment. But it is possible for the most widely renowned expert to be wrong sometimes, even about his or her own subject.

In the months and years to come, you will likely be exposed to a wide range of opinions, ideas, and beliefs about writing. Teachers, critics, friends, relatives, books, articles, and lecturers will all have things to say, and some will have things to say about your writing in particular. Some of these people will contradict one another, or even themselves. Some will present their opinions as facts.

Take the words of all these people with a grain of salt. Much of what they say will be helpful—but some of it may be misguided, inappropriate, or plain wrongheaded.

This doesn't mean to mistrust everyone or to ignore what teachers, critics, or other writers have to say. You should neither accept someone's ideas and judgments blindly nor ignore them blindly. This holds true whether that person is your spouse, your grandfather, a writing instructor, your favorite author, or the president of the Author's Guild.

When someone gives you criticism or advice, listen to it carefully. Don't try to argue with it, defend yourself, or prove the person wrong. Simply listen attentively and courteously. (You may, of course, ask for details or clarification.)

Then consider those comments carefully. Judge each comment or criticism separately, on its own terms, regardless of who said it or how sure or emphatic he or she was about it.

If a piece of criticism or advice makes sense, follow it. If it doesn't, ignore it. Use what is useful and reject what isn't. You don't have to explain to anyone why you haven't taken his or her advice, and you don't have to feel guilty or anxious about it.

Everything in this chapter applies to the contents of this book. It also applies to your own ideas and opinions about writers and writing.

35

Looking Back on What You've Done

BY NOW YOU'VE likely read the first thirty-four chapters of this book and tried out at least several of the exercises. Now it's time to look over what you've written.

Reread each of the pieces of writing you've created so far. Then, referring back to the pieces as often as you wish, ask yourself the following questions:

1. What images—sights, sounds, smells, etc.—occur or reoccur in these pieces? Do any categories of images (such as buildings, animals, or things underground) appear frequently?

2. Do particular people, or aspects of people, appear frequently?

3. What emotions do these pieces evoke? Which of these reoccur? Which reoccur regularly?

4. Does any theme or subject appear in more than one piece?

5. Does any setting appear in more than one piece?

THE ANSWERS TO these questions will give you some clues as to what your unique interests and materials are as a writer. If, say, ice cream keeps appearing in your work, you might want to consider what ice cream means to you. Is it a reward? A gift? A symbol of—or substitute for—parental love? Do the words "ice cream" evoke any strong images, ideas, or feelings in you? What is it about ice cream that attracts or intrigues you? (It may, of course, simply be that you love the taste of ice cream; but it is a good idea to look for other meanings and connections.)

Next recall the processes you went through to write each of these pieces. Where, when, and under what circumstances did you write? How long did each piece take? Did you write each piece in one sitting, or in two or more? How much rewriting was necessary? Did you use a pen, a pencil, a computer, or a typewriter? If you used more than one, which was most comfortable, and which produced the best results? Did you write each piece from beginning to end, or did you write the sections out of sequence? How often did you write and for how long at a stretch? The answers to these questions will begin to tell you what circumstances and processes work best for your own writing.

Now consider how well each piece turned out. Which ones are you happiest with? Least happy? Which ones still need work? Do you see any growth or improvement between your first pieces and your most recent ones? It's too soon to make any definitive judgments, but you will likely see some development.

Next, count the number of pages and pieces you've written. Then congratulate yourself.

Finally, ask yourself how you feel about writing so far. Has it been pleasurable? Rewarding? Thrilling? Boring? A pain in the behind? What have been its high points? Low points? Has it all been worth it? Do you want to continue? (If you realize that you *don't* want to write after all, don't feel guilty or disappointed. Instead, feel free to explore other potential interests, secure in the knowledge that you've given writing a reasonable try. And if you later change your mind and want to try writing again, that's fine, too. Hang onto this book just in case.)

Now you're ready to go more deeply into the craft, art, and process of writing.

36

A Few Unkind but Well-Deserved Words About Literature

LITERATURE IS NOTHING more (or less) than very good writing.

Writers and readers alike often forget that all works of literature—from the plays of Shakespeare to the novels of Hemingway to the poems of Adrienne Rich—were written by members of the same species as ourselves. What we call "literature" is no different in form, genesis, or content than what we call "creative writing." Indeed, some of the creative writing of today will become the literature of tomorrow.

Many of us have been taught—or, rather, mistaught—that literature is meant primarily to be studied, examined, analyzed, or torn apart. This is utterly untrue. Like all good writing—and like all good art—the purpose of literature is to move people and give them pleasure. The greatest literature is great precisely *because* it moves us greatly and gives us great pleasure.

Many of us were taught in high school to find hidden or secret meanings in certain stories and novels. But few serious writers hide secret meanings that readers are supposed to hunt down and dig up. This would be a scavenger hunt, not literature. The point of reading James Joyce or Grace Paley or Robert Frost or Shirley Jackson is to share (or absorb) an emotional experience that each author has to offer—not to vivisect each piece of writing to find out what makes it tick.

Not that there's no point to vivisection. You can learn a good deal about writing by pulling apart a literary work and examining it closely with a writer's (and critic's) eye. In fact, this is what literature scholars and literary critics do for a living. But few writers, and even fewer writers of great literature, wrote for these people. Rather, they wrote for men and women like you and me—people who read primarily for enjoyment.

It does you more harm than good to hold great literature, and the writers of great literature, in awe. These writers were human beings just like you and me. And they did exactly what you and I do when we write. They just did it better.

And in some cases, they didn't even do it better. Some of the supposedly great works of literature strike most readers today as thoroughly dull. Do you know anyone who enjoyed *Silas Marner* enough to read it a second time, just for fun?

It will do you no good as a writer to defer your judgment about literature to the "experts." There is room for taste, and even outright disagreement, in literature. Indeed, there currently exist (and have always existed) major disagreements about particular works, and about literary theory in general, within literary circles.

If you cannot make your own judgment about whether a work of literature is great, or merely good, or downright awful, how will you adequately judge your own stories and poems?

Feel free to judge each literary work on its own, regardless of who wrote it, what other people say and think about it, and what kind of a reputation it has. If you hate something, or if it bores you, don't try to argue yourself out of your reaction. Admit that you hate it or find it unbearably dull.

And if that's your genuine reaction to something *you've* written, admit that freely, too.

37

The Importance of Conciseness and Simplicity

THE BEST WAY to say anything is to say it as simply, straight-forwardly, and briefly as possible. This is true both when you speak and when you write.

This doesn't, however, mean to oversimplify. If Herman Melville had written, "A man wants badly to kill a whale named Moby Dick; he tries repeatedly but fails," that sentence wouldn't have lasted until today—and it surely can't replace Melville's novel. The trick is to write lines and sentences that get across every *necessary* detail and nuance, but that do so as simply and concisely as possible.

In some cases—for example, in a piece where imagery and rhythms play large roles—the simplest way may nevertheless be rather elaborate. However, it remains essential not to add any *unnecessary* images or rhythms, or the reader will drown in a sea of perfume.

If it's important to show a sea of yellow flowers in your piece, by all means give your reader that image. But don't write about an endless sea of stark yellow flowers, unless both "endless" and "stark" serve some worthwhile purpose.

The same principle applies to choosing individual words. Don't write "She ambled down the street" when "She walked down the street" will do as well. (Actually, it will do better, because it's simpler.) But if it's important that she amble rather than walk, by all means say "ambled." "She said" is usually better than "She expostulated" or "She remarked." And avoid using "He chuckled" or "He laughed" when actually he had been *speaking*. He can laugh in the next sentence.

If, in a poem, you want to get a character down the stairs and out the door, you should simply say, "She went downstairs and out the door"—or, perhaps better, "She left." If it's important or significant (though perhaps subtly or subliminally) that the door be old and made of oak, however, "She left" won't be sufficient. You'd need to say, instead, "She left and closed the old oak door." There could be any number of reasons why "old" and "oak" might be important: to establish the age of the house; to symbolically show weight, age, and solidity; to repeat an image of doors or trees that appeared earlier in the poem; or even to repeat the sound of the letter "o." All of these are legitimate—but no reason at all is not.

Sometimes you'll want to add an image or detail (or even a whole stanza or scene) and not know why. If so, ask yourself if it's genuinely necessary. If your gut tells you it is, even if you don't understand or can't explain why, use it. But if the piece can do without it without losing any of its power or effect, then it *should* do without it. Cut it out.

38

The Importance of Clarity

LANGUAGE SHOULD ALWAYS be as clear and specific as possible. Avoid jargon or vagueness. Don't say "I got in my vehicle" when what you mean is "I got in my car"—unless, perhaps, the character is a police officer making a report.

The same is true of obscurity. ("Obscure" means "little-known," "little-used," "unclear," or "unintelligible.") Always avoid obscure words and allusions. However, you may use *difficult* words or allusions when they are appropriate. There is no need to restrict yourself to a third-grade vocabulary.

Some new writers have the idea that obscurity is a plus rather than a minus. Some even think that good literature, particularly poetry, *should* be obscure.

This is very far from the truth. Think about it for a minute. Is it possible to enjoy a piece *because of* unintelligibility or lack of clarity? A reader who enjoys the unintelligible is not a reader worth having. (Such readers often think, "If I can't understand something, it must be deep and meaningful and therefore great art." These readers are simply being foolish.)

It's important not to confuse obscurity with ambiguity. Ambiguity can often be used to add power or depth to a piece of writing; but obscurity can only weaken it. In Philip Roth's *Zuckerman Unbound,* for example, when Zuckerman's brother Henry calls him selfish, cold-hearted, and uncaring, does he genuinely mean it, or is Henry merely upset from attending their father's funeral? It could be either, or both—most likely both. This ambiguity strengthens the scene. But if Roth had simply obscured Henry's feelings, we'd likely have no scene at all—and certainly no successful one.

It is just as important to avoid stilted or unnecessarily formal language. Use plain, everyday English unless something else is called for. *Don't* try to write in "Shakespearian" English or some other supposedly classy variation. Shakespeare's use of language may sound grand and eloquent now, but it was the everyday English of his own time.

Chapter 75 discusses other aspects of word choice.

I once had a writing student who believed that all poetry had to be written in pseudobiblical language. She insisted on using "thou" instead of "you," "art" instead of "are," and so on. No matter how many times I assured her that this was neither necessary nor helpful, she wouldn't believe me. One day she turned in a poem criticizing her ex-boyfriend. In it was this line: "For thou art the biggest geek." It taketh one to knoweth one, in my opinion.

39

Getting Your Readers to Use Their Senses

EACH OF US perceives the world through his or her senses. In fact, our senses are the only mechanisms we have for perceiving external reality.

When you write, you are in essence creating made-up worlds for your reader to temporarily believe in and live in. (If you are writing nonfiction, then you are *recreating* the world we already live and believe in.) To do either of these well, you must give your reader sensory information.

Ideas, thoughts, and principles make for good conversation, but in a work of fiction or poetry they aren't enough. To make your reader feel, you have to give him or her sights, sounds, smells, tastes, and "touches." All of these are called *images*. (In everyday language the word "image" refers only to the sense of sight; most writers and writing teachers use it to refer to all the senses.)

Below are two lists of words. What do the words in both lists have in common? What sets the two lists apart?

high-pitched	delightful
chalky	thrilling
sweet	disgusting
heavy	ugly
green	lovely
sharp	tremendous

vibrating	unbelievable
pungent	awful
rough	terrific
shiny	silly
squirming	attractive
thunderous	superb

All of the words above are adjectives. The words on the left are sensory words. They provide specific images—information about how things are. The words on the right express *judgments*; they tell the reader nothing about how or what something actually is. If I tell you I have a "lovely" object at home, can you describe it at all or even have the vaguest idea what it might be? But if I tell you I have a glass vase of tall, yellow lilies, can you see it?

Which of these sounds more appetizing: "freshly caught, charcoal-broiled salmon" or "a very good meal"?

When you use specific sensory images, you make people, places, and events come alive in your reader's mind. This enables him to make his own judgments, and—more importantly—to react and to feel. But merely telling your reader that something is "wonderful" or "hideous" or "beautiful" keeps him from sensing anything—and, ultimately, from feeling anything.

This doesn't mean that you should never use the words in the right-hand list, or words like them. But if you do find yourself using such words, ask yourself if sensory details would be more useful.

Nor does this mean that the more sensory details, the better. Don't forget the importance of simplicity. What brings a scene, setting, or situation to life is not a profusion of details, but a few that are just right. Often the combination of two or more different senses will make everything click for your readers. (For example, imagine the smell of suntan lotion combined with the burning of hot sand on the bottoms of your feet.)

40

Showing vs. Telling

GOOD WRITING REVEALS rather than explains. A successful story or poem—or, for that matter, a successful line, sentence, stanza, or paragraph—shows the reader what is happening rather than merely tells him or her about it.

Compare these two sentences: "Jenny was angry." "Jenny bit her lip and slammed the book shut." Which sentence makes you want to keep reading? Which is more moving? Which is more vivid?

The first sentence shows the reader nothing. It's devoid of sensory information. It merely explains how Jenny feels.

The second sentence, however, *reveals* Jenny's anger through two specific sensory details: the sight of her biting her lip and the sight—and sound—of her slamming the book closed. These images enable us to actually *see* her anger and, more importantly, feel it.

Note that nowhere in the second sentence does the word "anger" appear. We don't need to be told that she's angry because the sentence shows us her anger clearly. (The biting of her lip also implies that she's trying to hold some of her anger back.)

When you write, don't tell your reader *about* things: "It was awful." "I feel great." "I couldn't believe my eyes." Instead, *show* him or her exactly what's happening, moment by moment, detail by detail: "The bottle had fallen off the coffee table and shattered, spilling wine and glass shards across the yellow carpet." "I felt the wind blow through my hair and couldn't keep from smiling." "She handed Tony the tiny silver pendant, and he clasped it tightly in his fist."

Whether you write prose or poetry, the principle is the same: let your reader *experience* an event or image, as if he were living through it himself. Give him the same sensory information, the same details, that he would notice (and find important) if he were actually there.

Explanations are no substitute for experience. If you have a box of cookies, experience is eating the cookies inside; explanation is merely reading the label.

EXERCISE #9

WRITE A PIECE that involves one of the following pairs:

> A death and a coat
> A mountain and a light
> A house and a scent

THINGS TO KEEP in mind:

- If you want to write about a death and a house, or a mountain and a scent, etc., go ahead.
- Feel free to use any definition of any of these words that you like. The coat can be a coat of paint; the house can be a birdhouse; and so on.
- Events or objects can appear "off stage." For example, you might speak of someone having just purchased a house, rather than actually showing a house, in your piece.

41

What Does It Mean to Understand a Piece of Writing?

IT IS POSSIBLE to enjoy a piece of writing without understanding it fully. This is true whether you're reading or writing it. Indeed, writers don't always fully "understand" their own work, either while they're writing it or after it's completed.

The truth is that understanding and appreciating a literary work (or any work of art) are two different things. In fact, understanding a piece isn't always the point.

I can understand the Dick and Jane books perfectly well, but that doesn't make them interesting to me, and it certainly doesn't make them literature. On the other hand, I don't "understand" Salvadore Dali's paintings at all, but I like them very much. Nor do I understand Robert Coover's short story "The Babysitter"—even though it's one of my favorite stories.

In fact, neither Coover's story nor Dali's paintings are *supposed* to be "understood" in the usual sense of the word. They are meant to be experienced, absorbed, and—most important—enjoyed and savored.

The word "understand" can be misleading. If you can experience and enjoy a work of art, then you actually *do* understand it, though not necessarily in a logical or intellectual way. Sometimes your gut, or your subconscious, or the right side of your brain understands something that the logical parts of you just don't "get." This is exactly how surrealist and cubist art works.

Indeed, when you write, the point isn't to make your reader understand. The point is to make him or her feel.

42

You Can Pick Your Friends, But You Don't Have to Pick a Style

SOME WRITERS, SUCH as Henry James, e. e. cummings, and Ernest Hemingway, have unique and easily recognizable writing styles. Other writers, such as Eudora Welty and E. L. Doctorow, alter their styles from one piece to the next, depending on the particular effects they wish to achieve. Which option is better?

Neither, of course. Or, rather, it depends on your own unique development as a writer. If you find yourself building a style (or even several different styles) of your own, fine. But if you find yourself becoming a chameleon, able to change styles at will, that's fine, too. The benefit of a single style is that your published work is more easily recognized and remembered; the benefit of multiple styles is the flexibility they afford you in theme, tone, and approach.

Although you are free to deliberately develop a single style of your own—or to stretch your talents by working with multiple styles—it is not necessary to approach the issue so systematically. Writers' styles and ranges tend to develop more or less naturally. You can learn a great deal about your own style(s) and range simply by looking back on what you've written so far.

Some writers—and some readers—feel that developing a unique, recognizable style is an important part of a writer's career and represents a form of literary maturity. This simply isn't true. It is possible to be a poor writer whose work is quite immature, yet still possess a unique (and even intriguing) literary style—just as it is possible to have no special style at all, yet be a master at writing.

43

Other Things You Don't Have to Pick

NEW WRITERS OFTEN search for—or try to build—their own literary identities. They may do this by developing particular styles; or they may select a particular approach (e.g., feminism), technique (e.g., regular use of the present tense), genre (e.g., fiction), subgenre (e.g., science fiction), or message (e.g., organized religion is dangerous but necessary).

Again, you are free to deliberately choose any of these you like—but you don't have to. If you want to write a sonnet about building a doghouse, then a suspense story, then an article on Winston Churchill, then three poems about lumberjacks, that's perfectly fine.

Some writers feel safer and more in control when they set certain limits for themselves. This is quite acceptable, and even reasonable, for a new writer. But after a year or two, you should begin stretching your abilities and trying new things. You have nothing to lose by trying except some time and energy—and a great deal to gain.

Some writers choose particular subgenres, techniques, or approaches for professional reasons: to reach a specific and fairly cohesive readership (horror fans, for example), to stand out immediately from other writers, or to build a career quickly. There is some sense to this, but there is just as much sense to the opposite route. If you allow yourself to work with a wide range of topics, genres, techniques, and approaches, you offer editors many more choices, and your chances of getting something (or many things) published may be much greater. Sticking to narrow limits can do a lot for a writing career—*if* those limits click with editors. If they don't, you may be up the proverbial creek without a paddle. (For more information on the professional side of writing, see chapters 89-90 and 95-97.)

44

Metaphor and Symbolism

IN CHAPTER 36 I explained how absurd it is to hunt for secret meanings when you read. This doesn't mean, though, that metaphors, symbols, and double- and triple-meanings don't appear in good writing, because they do all the time. But all of these things arise naturally and spontaneously in our writing, just as they do in our dreams and waking fantasies. Indeed, symbols, metaphors, and multiple meanings are constant parts of our everyday lives. Once you begin looking for them in your life, you'll see them everywhere. (And you won't be making them up; they're really there.)

Symbols and metaphors may be used often and well. But they are not obligatory; some of the best stories and poems are wholly devoid of symbol and metaphor.

You *can* use metaphors and symbols quite deliberately in your writing. But they should not be puzzles to assemble or strings of clues to hunt down. They should naturally augment the effect of your piece; your reader should not need to go deliberately looking for additional meaning or implication.

An excellent example is Dylan Thomas's story "The Peaches," in which two families meet. One is sophisticated and upper class, the other an unsophisticated farm family. The story centers around the lives of two boys—one from each family—who spend part of a summer together at the poor family's farm. In the story, a can of peaches—considered the greatest of treats by the farm family and the tawdriest of foods by the sophisticates—represents the very different ways in which the two families live and view the world. But the peaches are not meant to be taken *primarily* as a symbol—they are, first and foremost, actual peaches. You can miss the symbolism completely and still understand and enjoy the story, because the entire piece shows in detail how the two different families act and think. If Thomas had left the peaches out of his story entirely, it would still be a success, though not quite as large a one. (It also, of course, would have a different title.)

This is how metaphor and symbolism work. They *augment* the events and imagery in a piece of writing. They do not— and should not—replace them.

45

"Shep Shall Bark No More"

THERE ARE TWO subjects that new writers almost invariably gravitate toward, especially in their very first stories and poems. These topics are chosen so very often that they have been given these official names by writing teachers: The Death of a Dear Small Animal, and My Profound Sexual Experience.

I have likely put my finger on one or two of the things you have recently written about, or were planning to write about, perhaps even in response to one of the exercises in this book. If so, there's no need to be embarrassed. There's nothing wrong with writing on either topic.

However, because these two subjects are such regular favorites of new writers, chances are very slim that your own stories or poems on these topics are unique or fresh. Your account of Shep's last days or the story of the loss of your virginity may thrill you, but I seriously doubt if anyone else will be moved by either one, simply because both themes have been handled over and over and over—possibly by everyone who has ever touched pen to paper. Writing teachers are particularly jaded, as we see three to six new dead pet pieces every term.

None of this means that you shouldn't write about either subject if you want to. But you should avoid showing these pieces to others, particularly if you want criticism—because the criticism is almost guaranteed to be negative. *Never* judge your writing ability or progress by these pieces, and never let anyone else make such a judgment.

It should go without saying that Dead Animal and Profound Lovemaking pieces ought not to be sent to editors for publication.

EXERCISE #10

WRITE A PIECE that takes place in a waiting room.

THINGS TO KEEP in mind:
- Part of the piece may take place in another location, or in several other locations.
- The waiting room can be in any location you choose.
- If you like, you can define "waiting room" as any room or area where one or more people wait for something—for example, the living room where a husband waits for his wife to get home, or the chapel where the wedding guests wait for the bride to enter.

46

Art vs. Entertainment: Some Useful Words on an Old Debate

ABOUT TEN YEARS ago, a book was published with this subtitle: *Stories to Read for Pleasure*. When I first saw the book I was taken aback: who in the world, I thought, reads for pain? Then I realized what the subtitle was meant to convey: "This book isn't art, it's *fun*."

Somewhere in our past, our literary and educational forefathers (and foremothers) got the idea that because art is Good For You, it must also be painful. Therefore, if it's pleasurable, it must be something less (or at least other) than art.

This is, of course, thoroughly ridiculous. Art not only can be pleasurable, it *ought* to be pleasurable—even fun.

I've also been witness to debates on literary works based on the question, "Is it art, or is it mere entertainment?" First of all, we need to admit that the two are not opposites—a story or poem is not either art *or* entertainment. If it is any good, it must *at least* be entertaining. If it is more than merely entertaining, it may also be art. Art *is* entertainment, and more.

Actually, I wonder if the question of art vs. entertainment is an important one at all. Suppose I write a poem that is entertaining but that falls short of being art. Is that so bad? Am I obliged to go back and somehow make it into art? Of course not—though I can if I want to.

In practice, I doubt if any serious writer ever sits down and says, "Today I will write a work of art" or "Today I will write something that is merely entertaining." The creative process doesn't work that way. Writers say what they need or want to say; sometimes it turns out as art, sometimes as mere entertainment, and sometimes somewhere in between.

Indeed, there is no hard and fast line between art and entertainment. They are parts of a continuum—a continuum that includes boredom. It looks like this:

$$\longleftarrow \hspace{7cm} \longrightarrow$$

Boring   Entertaining   Art

What's the best way to deal with this whole question? Ignore it and keep writing.

47

Dreams as Inspiration

YOUR DREAMS REVEAL what you think, feel, and care about, just as your thoughts and emotions do in your waking life. So why not put your dreams to work in your writing? You can use them just as you would your conscious observations: simply make note of the images, scenes, settings, situations, ideas, and entire dreams that interest or intrigue you.

The hardest parts of using your dreams are remembering them and writing them down. But you can learn to do both with a little practice. Here's what you do:

Keep a notebook and a pen or pencil right next to your bed, within easy reach. A tape recorder will also work well. Typewriters and computers are not recommended; whatever you use, you'll need to be able to reach over and pick it up quickly and easily, without disturbing the dream images that remain in your mind.

As soon as you wake up in the morning—not after you get out of bed, but the moment you regain consciousness—pick up the notebook or tape recorder. Try to recall the previous night's dreams. Write down (or dictate) everything you can remember: events, people, situations, images, details, feelings, settings, predicaments, and so on. It is very important that you do this immediately upon waking, when the night's dreams are still in your mind. If you wait even twenty or thirty seconds, the memories may slip away.

If, when you wake, you remember two or more dreams, or many details of a single dream, you may want to begin by jotting down a few of the most important items, so that while you're noting one dream, the other (or a different portion of that same dream) doesn't fade away.

It is best if you wake up without any distractions around you. It may be useful, therefore, to wake up fifteen minutes before the rest of your household. Lots of activity first thing in the morning can cause memories of dreams to vanish before you can get them down on paper.

When you do awaken, don't lunge for your notebook or tape recorder; instead, reach for it slowly, trying not to disturb your state of mind. If you can, keep your eyes closed until you are ready to begin writing or dictating.

If you have an image or memory in your mind as you wake up, deliberately hold onto it. If it starts to slip away, repeat it to yourself until you write it down.

Some of our most vivid and revealing dreams occur midway through the night. Some writers, therefore, like to make notes on their dreams every time they wake up for a moment, even if it's at 3 A.M. to go to the bathroom.

Using these techniques, you should be able to remember and write down at least some of your dreams. If they don't work for you, however, try setting your alarm for odd hours. Get up an hour earlier or later than normal, or wake yourself up once in the middle of each night.

If an image, person, scene, setting, or event appears regularly in your dreams, this is something especially worth exploring in your writing, because its recurrence means that it's of continued significance or importance to you.

However, it's not necessary to analyze your dreams, or understand what they mean, to use them in your writing. You may analyze them, or have someone analyze them for you, if you like. But you don't need to know what your dreams are telling you in order to use them to move your readers.

48

Fantasy and Daydreams as Inspiration

ALL OF US fantasize and daydream every day. So why not make use of your fantasies and daydreams in your writing, just as you can with your dreams?

The procedure is the same: when you find yourself fantasizing, write down the important details, events, people, images, situations, settings, ideas, and feelings. Some writers keep their journals, or pen and paper, with them at all times so they can make notes on their daydreams no matter where they are.

There is one major difference between dreams and waking fantasies: you can control your fantasies.

Most fantasies are about the best thing that could happen in certain circumstances, or the worst, or the scariest, or the strangest or funniest or most appropriate or most inappropriate or most ironic or most unexpected. Any of these can provide terrific material for a story or poem.

In addition to fantasies that arise spontaneously, you can try *deliberately* imagining what might happen. In any given situation, real or imaginary, explore one or more of the possibilities in the previous paragraph, and see what your mind comes up with. You may surprise yourself. This is exactly how I get some of my own best material.

You may, of course, modify a fantasy or daydream as much as you like. Indeed, I'll often take a fantasy, change

141

one or more of its elements, then begin fantasizing again. Sometimes I'll run the same daydream, with variations and modifications, through my head several times. Once in a while, in this manner, I'll plot out a whole story without even trying.

EXERCISE #11

IF YOU HAVE not yet read chapters 47 and 48, do so now.

Using the techniques described in chapter 47, record your dreams for a week or two. If an entire dream affects you emotionally, write down that whole dream. If only one part or image of a dream affects you, it is enough to write down only that part or image.

Next, spend some time deliberately daydreaming and fantasizing. Use the techniques outlined in chapter 48. Write down any images, scenes, or whole fantasies that move or intrigue you.

Now look over your notes for a few minutes.

Then use one or more of the ideas, images, or events from your dreams or waking fantasies (or both) as the basis for a story, a poem, or some other piece of creative writing.

THINGS TO KEEP in mind:

● If, during your waking fantasies, you hit a point where you know exactly how to start a piece of writing, go ahead and begin writing immediately.

● Likewise, if you wake up from a dream and know immediately what you want to write, don't wait. Begin writing.

● If a dream or daydream feels complete or self-contained —that is, if it needs no modification, expansion, embellishment, or elaboration to become a good poem or story—feel free to write it up exactly as you dreamed or fantasized it.

49

The Seven Major Forms of Creative Writing

THERE ARE SEVEN basic forms that creative writing can take:

The Novel
An extended piece of fiction, normally 40,000 words or more, usually but not necessarily building to a climax (and usually a resolution) near the end. A novel may have as few as two characters or over a hundred. (It's possible to write a novel with a single character, but I've never seen one.) The vast majority of novels have one major plot and one or more subplots.

The Essay
Includes reviews, news and feature stories, biography, memoirs, and all other forms of nonfiction prose. This book is a collection of very short essays, all closely related.

The Short Story
A work of fiction that is briefer than a novel or novella, usually based on a single plot or event. A story normally has

a climax and a resolution. Most short stories have few or no subplots and less than ten characters, though a few successful ones have been written with dozens of characters and quite a few subplots, and a few good stories have no characters or plot at all.

The Poem
Includes all forms of rhymed and unrhymed verse in all lengths. Specific forms include villanelles, sonnets, rondels, sestinas and haiku. (See chapter 87 for descriptions of these forms.)

The Play
A script, of any length, intended for performance by live actors before a live audience.

The Electronic Script
Includes scripts of all lengths for television, film, video, radio, and filmstrips. These works are meant to be recorded and edited; they are not intended for live performance.

The Song
A work of prose or poetry, of any length, intended to be sung. Includes ballads, gospel, rock 'n roll, and Gregorian chants.

It is of course possible for a piece to fit more than one of these categories. Shakespeare's dramatic works, for example, are both stage plays and poetry. A novel can be written in verse.

The great majority of literary works composed today fit one or more of these seven categories. But there are other, lesser-known, and less-used literary forms. Turn to the next chapter and see.

50

Other Forms of Creative Writing

HERE ARE SOME other contemporary genres:

The Prose Poem

A very brief piece of prose, usually under five hundred words, in which imagery and/or rhythms and sounds are of great importance.

The Short-Short Story

A very short story, normally under a thousand words, with a surprise (and often ironic) ending. The term "short-short" is sometimes used by magazine and anthology editors to refer to any story of less than fifteen hundred or two thousand words.

The Novella

A mid-length work of fiction, longer than a short story and shorter than a novel—usually about 20,000-35,000 words. Also called the *short novel*. Like a novel, a novella usually has some complexity in plot and characterization, one or more subplots, and a climax.

The Vignette

A brief work of prose, usually but not necessarily fiction, that clearly depicts a single event, setting, and/or person. A vignette need not (and normally does not) have a climax or resolution. The term SLICE OF LIFE is synonymous.

Creative Prose

This literary term currently has two different definitions: 1) A piece of fiction, often humorous, written in essay form—e.g., Woody Allen's "Exploring Psychic Phenomena" or Jorge Luis Borges's "The Babylon Lottery." 2) Any work of prose, other than a novel, novella, or short story, that is creative rather than (or as well as) reportorial—e.g., Annie Dillard's *Pilgrim at Tinker Creek* or the work of John McPhee. The term "creative nonfiction" is synonymous with this second definition. Although the term "creative prose" is new, people have been writing both forms of it for centuries.

The Novelette

Not a literary form at all but a term used by some editors and publishers to refer to a short story longer than 7,500 or 10,000 words.

51

How to Say What You Want to Say

SUPPOSE YOU ALREADY know what you want to express or communicate in a piece of writing, but you don't know how to say it. Suppose you don't even know whether your piece should be a short story, a poem, a novel, or a TV script. What do you do? How do you select the proper form?

First, play your hunches. If you think or feel that a certain genre or form is likely to be most appropriate, try it. If it doesn't work out, try a different approach or genre. (Some writers deliberately write the same piece, or sections of the same piece, in two or more ways, then compare the different versions to see which works best. This is an especially common technique for sorting out whose point of view a story or scene will be told from.)

If your hunches don't pan out, try a process of elimination. Since writing should be as simple and direct as possible, start with the simplest and most direct forms. Try writing your piece first in prose; if the piece can be written as either fiction or nonfiction, try nonfiction first. If prose proves unsuccessful, try the script form; if this doesn't work out, try poetry. Attempt shorter lengths before longer ones: try writing a piece as a short story or essay before you try it out as a novel or nonfiction book.

It is always possible, of course, that *no* standard literary form will suit what you want to write. It may be that you'll have to invent an entirely new form or genre; this will likely be a difficult task, but by all means give it a try if you like. Or it may simply be that what you want to do is impossible or beyond your abilities—and that *no* genre will do the trick.

EXERCISE #12

SPEND A FEW days deliberately (but discreetly and tactfully) eavesdropping on other people's conversations—at your workplace, in restaurants, in the supermarket, at bus stops, and anyplace else in public or private. Write down any quotes that impress, intrigue, or amuse you. (You'll probably be surprised at how many you'll find.) Always keep a pen and paper with you for this purpose.

When you have accumulated ten or more of these, write or type them all up on a piece of paper. Look them all over for a few minutes.

Now, use one or more of the quotes as the basis or beginning of a piece of writing.

THINGS TO KEEP in mind:

• If you "overhear" a good quote at your own dinner table or in your own bedroom, go ahead and use it. If it comes out of your own child's mouth, or even out of your own, it's still fair game. However, each quote must be taken from an everyday situation—you may *not* use anything from movies, plays, TV or radio shows, ads, etc.

• If a quote inspires you immediately, or if you get an idea for a piece of writing before you have accumulated ten quotes, don't wait. Go ahead and begin writing immediately.

- If a series of quotes, or even a whole dialogue, impresses or moves you, great. Use all or part of it, as you wish.
- The quote that actually gets you writing does not have to appear in your piece at all.
- You may modify any quote as much as you wish.
- If your eavesdropping provides you with useful images as well as quotes, by all means note them down, and feel free to use them in your writing.

52

Creative Lying

IF YOU'RE WRITING a news story for a magazine or newspaper, you are of course obliged to stick to the facts; lying and faking it aren't allowed.

Fiction and poetry (and all other forms of creative writing) are different, however. The point of reading a creative literary work is not to be informed of facts, but to be moved and entertained. As a creative writer, you have the right to lie, to make up anything you want.

Most of us make a clear distinction between fiction and nonfiction: fiction is made up, and nonfiction is real. But actually there is no clear borderline between the two.

Think back to an episode in your life that was important to you, or that you still remember vividly. You could write up this episode as a piece of nonfiction. But what if you were to change some of the details and events to make the piece more intriguing? What if the dog that had barked at you had bitten you instead? What if instead of winning $50 in the state lottery, you'd won $50,000? What if the IRS had prosecuted instead of fined you?

Try taking a real situation or experience and twisting, embellishing, or extending it. Make it scarier, or sadder, or funnier, or happier, or more dangerous. Take what really happened and daydream about it using the techniques in chapter 48. Imagine what *could* have happened. What if things had gone as well—or as badly—as possible?

What's important about a work of creative writing is that it moves the reader; whether it's true or not is usually trivial, if not irrelevant. After you read a story by Grace Paley or Raymond Carver, do you ask, "Yeah, but did it really happen?" Of course you don't. Indeed, many excellent short stories happen to be accounts of actual events; there's nothing wrong with billing a work of nonfiction as a short story or novel if it reads like one. A story, after all, can be a true story.

You also have the option of doing the opposite. If you are writing something wholly imaginary, feel free to add images, details, quotes, or events from real life, just as you perceived or experienced them.

This combination of reality and fakery—what others have called literary embellishment or license and I call creative lying—often leads to some of the best and most moving pieces of writing. It is possible to turn virtually any incident into something worth reading with a little (or a lot) of creative lying. This is why some writing teachers are always telling their students, "You've got plenty to write about; just look at your own life."

One important note: once you've started embellishing or making things up, you can no longer legitimately call such a prose piece nonfiction. (in poetry, of course, this is not an issue. Like fiction, poetry is not expected to be true or factual.)

53

Active and Passive Language

THE ENGLISH LANGUAGE offers two ways to describe any action or event: actively and passively.

Here is an example of active language: "Shelly bought a loaf of bread." Here is the same event expressed passively: "The loaf of bread was bought by Shelly."

Another example of active language: "The dog retrieved the newspaper." Now, the passive version: "The newspaper was retrieved by the dog."

One more example. Active: "I recommend an oil change." Passive: "An oil change is recommended."

Active language is almost always preferable to passive. It's more vibrant and energetic; it evokes clearer, sharper, and more effective images; it usually sets up better rhythms; and it's almost always simpler and more concise.

Most people who use passive language regularly don't realize they're doing it or that there's anything wrong with it. If you do have such a habit, you should recognize and break it as soon as possible. This will do a lot for your writing.

At first you will need to catch passive language as you rewrite. With experience, you'll be able to catch yourself as you write it. Eventually the use of active language will come naturally.

Active language is preferable to passive not only in creative writing, but in everything you write—letters, newspaper articles, and even thank-you notes.

One important note: there *are* times when passive language is more appropriate than active—though there aren't many of them. Feel free to use the passive *when you have good reason to do so.* (For example, if you have a maid dusting furniture and you want your reader to focus on a chair and not the maid, you might write, "In the center of the room was a tall green recliner, which was being dusted by the maid." This sentence also serves to emphasize the maid's subservient role.) Otherwise, stick with active language.

54

Three Tenses and Three Persons

HERE IS A quick review of some terms and their applications to writing:

Past Tense
The most common tense for both prose and poetry. Examples: "Richard jumped up." "It was late." "They had been busy."

Present Tense
Used occasionally in prose, fairly often in poetry. Examples: "I'm hungry." "She hands him the key." "He is very busy."

Future Tense
Rarely used in fiction and poetry, though certainly permissible and viable. Examples: "She'll be there on time." "The dog will stand on its hind legs." "You are going to be angry."

First Person
Anything in which the subject is "I" or "we." Examples: "I

bought a cup of tea." "I see her get into the cab." "We knew they were planning to surprise Ellen." Widely used in both fiction and poetry.

Second Person

Anything in which the subject is "you." Examples: "You'd better think again." "You will enter the room quietly." "You ate too much." Rarely used in fiction or poetry except in dialogue; however, it is possible and permissible to write a good second-person narrative.

Third Person

Anything in which the subject is "he," "she," "they," or "it." Examples: "He went home." "She'll meet him at the bank." "They don't like irises." "It's the best you can buy." Widely used in both poetry and fiction.

Every story or poem is written in a particular tense and person. (Some pieces change tense and/or person, perhaps even frequently. This is quite legitimate when done properly.)

Use of the present tense adds immediacy and intimacy. It can also be used to add suspense or tension. Use of the first person has similar effects.

Use of the second person adds mystery and intrigue. It can also add either a dictatorial, metaphysical, or omniscient flavor, depending on how it is used. Use of the future tense has similar effects.

Third person past is the simplest and most common combination in fiction and poetry. Next most common are, in order, first person past, first person present, and third person present.

First, second, and third person are *not* the same as point of view. See page 93 for details.

EXERCISE #13

WRITE A PIECE that begins with the words "If I took you" or "If I let you" or "If I showed you."

THINGS TO KEEP in mind:
- If you prefer to have those words appear somewhere other than at the beginning of your piece, that's fine.
- If you wish, instead begin your piece with the words "If you took me" or "If you let me" or "If you showed me."

55

Stream of Consciousness vs. Automatic Writing

"STREAM OF CONSCIOUSNESS" is a literary technique intended to simulate what goes on in a character's mind. Authors have used both standard English and nongrammatical variations to achieve this internal reality. Both techniques are quite sophisticated, require careful control (and often much rewriting), and are usually quite difficult to pull off. You are welcome to try your hand at a stream of consciousness piece if you like, but don't be too disappointed if the results are less than satisfactory or if the task is more than you can handle.

Simulating a character's thoughts and perceptions is very different from simply letting your own thoughts and perceptions—whatever comes into your head—flow onto the page in a steady stream. This, too, has been called stream of consciousness, but this is an incorrect use of the term. A more appropriate term might be "automatic writing."

Automatic writing can be very useful in providing raw material—images, ideas, short passages, etc.—for your writing. Automatic writing can also generate first drafts from which completed pieces can be developed. However, automatic writing will rarely, if ever, generate finished, polished work ready to publish or show to others. By all means try out automatic writing if you like, and use it if it proves helpful to you. But have no illusions that automatic writing will produce a "stream of consciousness" masterpiece.

Automatic writing done in verse form is sometimes mistakenly called "free verse." In truth, it is no such thing; it is still nothing more or less than automatic writing. *Real* free verse is poetry that has no regular rhyme or meter but that employs other poetic techniques. Automatic writing normally employs few or none of these techniques.

56

Bisociation

THE TERM "BISOCIATION" was coined by Arthur Koestler in his wonderful book *The Act of Creation.* It refers to the bringing together of two ideas or forces that would not normally be associated. Bisociation can result in strong images, ideas, events, or entire pieces.

Here are some examples of bisociation:

1) An advertising billboard on an alien spaceship.
2) A coat that makes you cooler instead of warmer, to be worn in summer.
3) An orientation guide to college for the *parents* of college students.
4) A corpse being kept cool in a supermarket dairy case.
5) A philosophy professor who moonlights as a tattoo artist.

Bisociation is one of the most important, and most basic, creative acts. It is one of the things that make good writing come to life.

The act of bisociation occurs naturally in all of us. But it is also possible to deliberately bisociate. Make a list of some images, ideas, situations, people, settings, and events that interest or intrigue you. Then try pairing them up in different combinations. (You may even want to put each item on a separate slip of paper and physically pair up the slips.)

I sometimes enjoy working with *tri*sociation—the uniting of *three* separate ideas or elements. I once wrote a story in which I brought together the city of Cleveland, surrealistic imagery from the paintings of Magritte and De Chirico, and the idea of an amusement park in the far future. The result was a Disneyland sort of theme park where robot bag ladies roamed the streets and the Cuyahoga River was set on fire every night at dusk for patrons' enjoyment.

Don't be afraid to use bisociation and trisociation in your own work.

EXERCISE #14

WRITE A PIECE about or involving one of the following:

Rock	Leaf
Fork	Fire
Coach	Stick
Sage	

THINGS TO KEEP in mind:

• You may use any legitimate definition of any word. For instance, "rock" can refer to rock music, the Rock of Gibraltar, a rocking cradle, Prudential Insurance, and so on.

• Don't simply describe a rock or a fork. There should be some point or significance to your piece; something should happen in it.

• Your rock, fork, or whatever does not need to be central to your piece. It can appear only in a single line or sentence if you wish.

Finding Your Ideal Critic

SOONER OR LATER you're going to want others to read at least some of what you've written. You'll probably also want some good criticism on your finished and/or unfinished work. How and where do you find a good critic, and what makes someone a good one?

First of all, someone who may be a good critic for one author (or one particular piece) may not be for another. A lot depends on what that piece or author is trying to achieve. Nor does someone have to be a reviewer, writing teacher, editor, English major, or another writer to be a decent critic. Indeed, a good critic need not have a background in literature at all, as long as he or she is intelligent. (It is also possible that someone who *does* have the "proper" background will be an inappropriate or worthless critic for a particular piece or author.)

The most important qualification of a critic for your work (or for one particular piece you have written) is that he or she be *generally* sympathetic to what you are trying to do. If you write a sonnet sequence and bring it to someone who hates rhymed poetry, you are not going to get a useful critique, even if that person has won a Nobel Prize in literature; he or she will probably critique your choice of form rather than your work itself.

If you've written a science fiction story, your ideal critic will need to like science fiction. If you've written an experimental prose poem lauding cats, your ideal critic will be someone who likes cats and who isn't afraid of nontraditional forms and approaches.

No piece of writing is going to appeal to everybody; any time you write any poem or story you are automatically selecting a limited audience to appeal to. Your ideal critic should represent the sort of reader you are trying to reach in that particular piece.

Where do you find such a person? You can of course contact a paid manuscript critic if you like; ads for many of these critics appear in the back of the magazines *Writer's Digest* and *Writer's Yearbook*. If you are enrolled in a writing class, you can approach your instructor and/or one of your fellow students; if you like, you can enroll in such a class just for this purpose. You also have the option of arranging an independent study project with an instructor in which he or she critiques your work.

Another possibility is joining or signing up for an existing writers' workshop, or starting a workshop of your own. (See chapter 96 for details.)

But it is often enough to simply find a friend or relative who thinks more or less like you do and whose opinion you respect. Almost any intelligent person who exemplifies the kind of reader you are trying to reach will do.

Here are the other qualifications of a potential critic:

• He or she must be willing to read your work carefully and offer honest reactions.

• He or she must be at least moderately literate and articulate.

• He or she must be willing to point out a piece's strong *and* weak points. (Be sure to specifically ask for both positive and negative comments. People have a tendency to offer only one or the other.)

• He or she must be able to discuss specifics—i.e., must be able to go beyond simply, "I liked it" or "I didn't like it."

A good critic can also see deeply into your own intentions, discuss those intentions with you, provide direction, and help you see and develop new approaches to your topic and/or material.

When you receive criticism from others, no matter who they are or what their relationship to you is, keep in mind the advice in chapter 34. Don't interrupt, contradict, or argue with your critic, and don't try to defend yourself or your piece. Listen carefully and consider everything you're told; then take what comments you find useful, and ignore the rest.

One good critic is usually enough at first, but feel free to find two, three, or even several if you can. Do keep in mind several things, however: critics can disagree; critics can be wrong (they can even all agree and all be wrong, though this is rare); you don't have to agree with a critic or do what he or she suggests; and, ultimately, the decision on what to write or how to write (or rewrite) it is always your own. (More details on multiple critics appear in chapter 93.)

Finding one or more good critics may take some trial and error—just like writing itself.

58

How to Spot and Ignore Bad Advice

THROUGHOUT YOUR TIME as a writer, people will give you tips and advice—in lectures, in person, and in books and magazines. Some of this advice will be unasked for. Much of it will be helpful; but much of it will be useless, or even harmful. How can you tell when advice is good and when it isn't?

There is no infallible test, of course. But here are some guidelines that should help:

• If advice or criticism feels right, or makes sense in your gut, it's usually worth following. (Note: this applies to criticism rather than compliments. Compliments tend to feel good even when they're unjustified.)

• Any comment that takes the form of "all writing must" or "all writers must" or even "all good writers must" is usually highly suspect. This also applies to more specific variations, such as "all love poems must" or "all mystery writers must."

• If someone makes a comment on your work that simultaneously compliments himself and/or his work, be very suspicious. This person may be more interested in puffing himself up than in helping you.

• Any appeal to authority should be ignored. Examples: "The editors at any good literary magazine would feel the same way." "Professor Smoot at Yale agrees with me." "It was unfavorably reviewed in *The New Yorker*." No one is ever right *because* he or she is an authority. This principle applies to both positive and negative comments on your work.

• Any appeal to consensus should be taken seriously but not followed blindly. If two or more readers say the same thing about a piece of writing, chances are good that what they have to say has some (and perhaps much) merit. But there is no guarantee of this: when James Joyce's work was first published, it was almost unanimously panned by critics.

• If a comment is vague or ambiguous, be sure to ask for an explanation or clarification.

59

Outlining, Netlining, and No Lining at All

CHANCES ARE THAT when you were growing up, at least one of your teachers told you, "Always make an outline before you write anything." You've also probably known some writers who swear by outlines—and some who never use them at all.

Outlining can be a useful tool, and you should use it whenever you like. However, it is by no means a necessity, and certainly not a requirement.

The term "outline" actually has many different meanings. Your high school or college teachers may have taught you to write what is called a *formal outline,* in which your topic and approach are broken down into headings, subheadings, and sub-subheadings (e.g., I, II, III, A, B, C, 1, 2, 3, a, b, c, i, ii, iii, etc.).

Then there are informal outlines that serve to keep information and ideas straight and available. These may take any useful or convenient form—lists, paragraphs, notes, synopses, etc.

Then there are "outlines" as defined by book publishers. These are tools by writers to describe and sell their unfinished books to editors. Outlines for nonfiction books can take any form that gives editors a clear picture of a book's form and content. Formal outlines, lists of general topics to be covered, narrative synopses of chapters, and annotated tables of contents have all been widely used. What book publishers call an "outline" for a fiction book, however, is invariably a narrative synopsis of the plot—an extremely condensed version of the book, usually written in present tense.

Any of the variations listed above can be useful, and you should feel free to use any one or more of them before you write, as you write, or even after you write. You may of course combine two or more outlining techniques or make up your own.

As you write, you'll learn for yourself when (and whether) to do up an outline, and what kind to use. In many cases no outline will be necessary; in others, a few basic notes may be sufficient; in others, you may find that only certain portions need outlining; and in still others, outlining may be necessary to save you from confusion, tangled subplots, and action that bogs down.

I rarely do much outlining in advance, but sometimes when I'm stuck on a scene or chapter, I find that stopping and outlining that particular section (and sometimes the whole piece) enables me to sort out my thoughts and write a much better draft. Sometimes I wind up outlining what events or material a section or piece will contain; other times I outline what I'm trying to achieve in each section or what purposes it is meant to serve. (Some writers find that outlining metaphor, intent, or symbolic movement is more important than outlining surface events or images.)

THERE IS ALSO a technique called *netlining* that many writers find extremely useful. An outline is usually a sequential list of items; a netline is a visual display of items and topics and how they interrelate or interconnect. A netline may or may not be sequential; most netlines look, and are used, something like flow charts. An example appears on the next page.

Meeting of narrator and lover at stream in spring.

He bends over to watch a pair of mating dragonflies.

He loses sunglasses in the stream. She retrieves them.

First date. They go to picnic by a lake. It starts to rain.

Image of water dripping off her nose and chin.

They get drunk. Should have brought jug of water and drunk some of that instead.

Narrator has sister who drowned seven years ago. Has same first name as lover.

Narrator had pulled body of sister from icy water.

Narrator tells lover of drowning.

WATER

The day they move in together the water on the block is shut off. They go to a motel to take a shower, but never get past the bed.

Final scene. Narrator walks through snow, finds the frozen stream where they met.

Has to put on sunglasses to keep from being blinded by glare off the snow.

ICE

Their first big argument is over something as silly as ice cubes: she accuses him of using them all and never refilling the tray.

Early winter. They go walking by same lake.

Lover falls through ice. Narrator catches her.

The heat of the argument makes them both realize how much tension was under the surface.

Breakup. Last meeting, at coffee shop.

They talk until coffee is cold and undrinkable.

171

This would be a netline for a poem in eight sections detailing a love affair from beginning to end. The chronology moves clockwise from the upper left through the lower left. Imagery of water and ice dominates the poem, and a fair amount of symbolism is used. (Examples: the lover's fall through the ice foreshadows the end of the romance; the snow blindness in the final section symbolizes the pain of loss and loneliness.)

As netlines go, this one is rather symmetric and sequential. Netlines are often much looser, much less logical, and much more cryptic in their notations. (In my netline, the poem is already pretty well thought through; often netlines are begun with very little material to go on, precisely for the purpose of thinking through and structuring a piece.) Some writers' netlines include dozens of items and interconnecting lines, and many of these items may consist of a single word, idea, or image.

Netlines may of course also be used for stories, novels, plays, and other literary forms.

All of these techniques are intended to help make your writing go more easily and smoothly. Use them (or ignore them) as you please.

EXERCISE #15

WRITE A PIECE that takes place in a hospital, a police station, bus stop, or cemetery. Part of the piece may take place elsewhere if you wish.

60

What Is a Draft?

MANY NEW WRITERS don't really know what a draft is. So, first, a definition: a draft is a complete, beginning-to-end version of a literary work. The first time you "write through" a piece you have created a first draft, the second time a second draft, and so on.

A lot of misinformation, misdirection, and guilt is connected with the concept of drafts. Very likely somewhere in your past one of your teachers insisted that you write at least three drafts of a particular paper. Other teachers (and even other writers) may have told you that every good story or poem needs at least two, or four, or six drafts. These ideas contain several invalid assumptions.

For starters, not everyone writes in drafts at all. Surely some writers sit down and write pieces through from start to finish time after time, but that's not how many (and perhaps most) writers do it. Many writers work in bits and pieces, one section or scene at a time; they may not move on to the next section until they've got the previous one right, or nearly right. Even those writers that do write from beginning to end time after time rarely find that every section needs exactly the same number of run-throughs.

Thus there is rarely such a thing as, say, the fourth draft of a piece. More typically, portions of that piece have been rewritten seven, eight, or nine times; other portions have been reworked two or three times; and still other portions remain more or less as they were written first time around. This very book was composed in just this way.

Furthermore, the notion that a story or poem should take a certain number of drafts (whether that number be one, four, or a hundred) is absurd. You should work on a piece until it feels finished (or until you choose to abandon it); sometimes this will mean a lot of work, sometimes comparatively little. More is not necessarily better; just as it's a mistake to declare a piece of writing finished before it genuinely is, it's a mistake to continue writing once a piece is done, even (indeed, *especially*) if it came quickly and easily in a single draft.

Indeed, why count the number of drafts at all (except, perhaps, to keep track of them), let alone try to write the correct number of them? Each new piece of writing is a new effort, a new challenge. Whether a piece is in its first, fourth, or eighteenth draft is irrelevant; whether it's any good or not is what counts.

One other misconception about drafts needs clearing up. Retyping a piece and making small changes here and there does *not* constitute writing a new draft. There is a major difference between rewriting and polishing. The next chapter will discuss this topic in detail.

61

Revising

WRITING WELL ALSO means revising and polishing your work well.

Revising (or revision) and rewriting are one and the same. They are the process of taking a new look at a piece of writing (or its subject, or a portion of that piece), then approaching it in a new or different way. ("Revision" means literally "to see again.")

Polishing—sometimes called editing—is a different process entirely. It presumes that what you have written so far is generally on target—that you don't need to take a fresh look at your piece or section. All that is needed are adjustments and some smoothing out of rough edges. It is possible for a piece of writing to require a good deal of polishing but no revision.

Proofreading is the process of checking for technical problems—omitted words, misspellings, improper punctuation, and so on. Proofreading is the final step in the polishing process.

Revising and polishing are fundamentally different, and you can't substitute one for the other. A piece that has a flaw in its conception cannot be fixed with any amount of polishing; it needs rethinking and rewriting.

REWRITING AND POLISHING should proceed from the largest concerns to the smallest. First you should ask yourself, "Is this piece generally doing what I want it to do? If not, why not, and how should I change it?" Once the piece is generally on track, then you need to look at each section and, if the piece has characters, at each character. Are they doing what they should for your piece? If not, rework them. The next step is to examine each stanza or paragraph: then each sentence or line; then each word; and, finally, spelling, grammar, punctuation, and other such details.

Rewriting (when it is necessary) should always precede polishing. Trying to fix the small things before dealing with the larger ones is tempting, but it puts the cart before the horse. Getting the rhythm just right in a line won't do you much good if the whole stanza needs rewriting.

Rewriting doesn't necessarily mean starting entirely from scratch. When I rewrite, I keep my previous version (and, if appropriate, several previous versions) in front of me. Then, as I write a new draft, I follow along in the old one(s), drawing from them phrases, sentences, and paragraphs that are worth keeping. Sometimes I'll combine elements from several different earlier versions to form a later one.

One writer I know rewrites for one specific item at a time. She'll go through once (or as many times as necessary) to get her characterization right; then she'll concentrate on dialogue; then metaphor, symbolism, and imagery; and so on.

ONCE YOU HAVE reached the polishing stage, you can begin to look at individual sentences and lines, at rhythms and pace, at matters of word choice, and so on. A piece (or section thereof) may require only a single round of polishing, or it may require several. Be willing to go through anything you've written as many times as necessary to get all the details right. Your last read-through should be a careful, final proofreading. Some writers proofread each of their pieces twice, or have someone else proof them. A new reader may spot errors your eye skipped over.

In your proofreading, be alert to previous changes. For

177

instance, if you changed a character's name or the color of his eyes, make sure the change is made throughout the piece.

Simplifying is an important part of both rewriting and polishing. You'll recall from chapter 37 that good writing is as simple, concise, and direct as possible. As you rewrite, polish, and proofread, simplify anything that is unnecessarily complex. (For example, don't write, "Joe walked down the street away from me" when "Joe walked away" or even "Joe left" will do just as well.) Also as you rewrite and polish, clarify anything that is unnecessarily vague, ambiguous, or unclear, and replace or get rid of any cliches.

It's quite common for a writer to feel that a piece is finished, only to read it again days, weeks, or months later and decide that it needs further revision or polishing. This is fine; go with that new decision. However, do keep in mind the tips in chapter 77 on knowing when a piece is really finished.

62

The Art of Cutting

ONE OF THE most important parts of both rewriting and polishing is what is called *cutting*—the deletion of unnecessary or inappropriate words, phrases, lines, paragraphs, stanzas, and scenes. Cutting can (and usually should) be done at every stage of revision and polishing.

In general, cutting is more of a problem for newer writers than for experienced ones, simply because new writers aren't used to doing it. But *most* writers, including most good ones, write too many words, repeat themselves, overstate their themes or imagery, and/or don't give their readers enough credit. The experienced writer therefore *expects* to find material in each of his or her pieces that needs to be cut, and makes those cuts quite willingly.

The two most important principles behind cutting are:

1) Get rid of anything and everything in a piece that doesn't support what the piece is doing.
2) Get rid of everything that isn't necessary.

Anything extraneous or redundant (from a word to half the piece) should go. Anything that harms your piece more than it helps it should also go. Any mere glitter—that is, anything that is pretty or clever but that does not really support the piece—should also go. And any cliches should be eliminated or replaced.

Cutting is often painful. Sometimes you'll realize that you have to get rid of some of your best lines, stanzas, or scenes because they really aren't important to that particular piece. Other times you'll realize you have to cut out the very portions you worked hardest on. Occasionally you may even find that your 10,000-word short story is really only a 600-word vignette, and that a single scene from that story does everything you wanted to do. In each of these situations, it's hard to get rid of all the good writing you worked so hard and long on—but grit your teeth and be merciless. Cut those sections out.

But don't throw them away! Though it may be necessary to remove sections from certain pieces, that doesn't mean you can't use them (or the ideas and images in them) elsewhere. In fact, you can use those excised sections (either rewritten or just as they are) to generate new stories and poems.

Occasionally I've started cutting a piece, only to realize that *the entire piece* should go: it says or does exactly what another one of my pieces says or does—or it does exactly what a published piece by another writer does. In these cases, I've simply filed those pieces away.

HERE ARE SOME other general tips on cutting:

• Cutting proceeds like rewriting and polishing, from the largest concerns to the smallest. First see if entire scenes or sections can go; then worry about stanzas or paragraphs; then about individual lines or sentences; then about single words or phrases.

• If you are having a problem with a section or a piece and can't figure out how to fix it—or if nothing you try seems to work—try simply cutting out that entire section. Most of the time this will work beautifully.

• As my eighth grade English teacher told me, "When in doubt, leave it out." That is, if you're not sure whether something should stay in or come out, usually it should be taken out.

180

EXERCISE #16

IF YOU HAVE not yet read chapters 59 through 62, do so now.

Take some time to look carefully through all the exercises you have written so far. Pick one that you like, and that you think can be turned into a successful piece, but that you feel needs work.

Keeping in mind what you have read about rewriting and polishing, do whatever you need to rewrite and complete that piece.

THINGS TO KEEP in mind:

• Although it is possible to do all the necessary additions, revisions, cuts, and polishing in a single sitting, it is more likely that you will need to return to the piece on several occasions to finish it completely.

• Feel free to try this process out on more than one exercise—or, if you prefer, on some piece of writing other than your responses to the exercises in this book.

63

Getting Unstuck

SOONER OR LATER—probably sooner—you are going to get stuck somewhere in a piece of writing and not know what to do next. This happens to most writers now and then.

I've already mentioned the two best ways to get unstuck: skip over the problem and come back to it later, or to cut the problem section out entirely. But there are plenty of other techniques that have helped writers unstick themselves; I'll make a list of some of the best ones below. Feel free to use any of them you wish, and/or to use methods of your own.

• Try starting that section, or even the whole piece, over again. If you get stuck again, try a different approach—perhaps a different point of view, a different time or setting, a different narrator, a different central image or metaphor, etc.

• Work on another project (writing or otherwise) for a while. Then come back to the problem piece.

• Retype or rewrite your last page, then keep going.

• Write a letter or something else that comes easily. Then return to your project.

• Change how, when, or where you write. Sometimes a change in circumstances can give you a fresh perspective. Trade in your typewriter for a pencil and pad; or try writing late in the evening instead of right after breakfast; or write in a library or coffee shop instead of in your bedroom.

- Make your circumstances for writing as comfortable as possible. Crank up the heat, or keep a thermos of hot chocolate next to your desk, or hook up a stereo in your office.

- Distract yourself. Take your mind *off* the piece and the problem. Go to a movie, take a walk, or read a book. Avoid writing anything at all for a few hours or days. Then, once you've truly forgotten about the problem for a while, go back to it.

- Put the piece aside for a while—a day, a week, or three months. Forget about it. Then return to it and see if you have any new ideas.

- Make a list of all possible solutions to your problem. Don't exclude *any* ideas, even if they seem absurd. If your intuition comes up with something, write it down. Then try out one or more of these ideas. If the best ones don't work, try some of the less promising or reasonable ones.

- Sit quietly for a few minutes, either concentrating on your own breathing or letting your mind wander. Then, gently, return your attention to the trouble spot. Don't try to come up with a solution; instead, simply see what bubbles up into your consciousness. Write these ideas down. When you've gotten all you think you're going to get, try some of them out. If some of them seem silly or absurd, try them anyway.

- Brainstorm with other people about your problem. (These people need not be writers.) Invite and consider fresh ideas, suggestions, and perspectives.

- Tell yourself you will work on the problem for one more hour (or half hour, or afternoon, etc.); then you'll quit for the day, whether you've solved the problem or not. Keep this promise to yourself.

- If you work well under pressure, set a *reasonable* deadline for solving the problem. Then stick to it.

- Keep writing, even if you're going nowhere. Let the piece wander or lose its way. Push ahead until something clicks.

- Promise yourself a reward of something you like very much once you've resolved the problem. Keep this promise.
- Think about your problem for a few minutes. Then try Exercise #24 from this book.
- Apply Exercise #8 from this book to your problem.
- Stop writing altogether for a while. Maybe all you need is some time to build up creative momentum.

64

One or More Good Turns

SOMETIMES A PIECE of writing will be technically competent, or even quite good, but nevertheless rather flat, dull, or uninspiring. Other times a piece won't quite hang together but you won't know why. Still other times the whole piece may seem strained, as if it's barely holding itself together.

All of these symptoms are often the result of a piece of writing that simply doesn't try to do enough, that is too thin or one-sided or simplistic.

One excellent solution to this dilemma is to take your piece one step further, to add to it an additional theme, idea, image, character, scene, stanza, extended metaphor, or plot-twist.

Imagine that your poem or story is the mainspring of a watch that isn't wound up quite tight enough. What you may need to do is wind it one or two turns tighter, by adding material or deepening what you already have. Bisociation and trisociation can prove especially helpful here. Look at what your piece is already doing; then ask yourself what else that same piece can do. What can make it stronger, meatier, and more moving without undercutting its original intent? Whatever ideas you come up with, try them out. The results will usually be good—often excellent.

EXERCISE #17

WRITE A PIECE that involves or makes use of three of the items below:

     A ball
     A flower
     A thunderstorm
     A flag
     A green house
     Fire

65

Creative Waiting

WRITING IS A creative act, not a mechanical one. Just about anyone can cook a hamburger when asked to, regardless of his or her mood, talent, or background. But few of us can write a good poem about hamburgers on demand; writing doesn't usually work that way. (There are exceptions, though; Chekhov was one of them. If you *can* turn out good writing any time you please, congratulations—you are one of the very few luckiest ones.)

Many writers, in fact, have a natural rhythm that includes periods of work and periods away from work. During these "off periods" they may still be observing, processing ideas and images, and subconsciously making connections; but they won't be putting many, or even any, words on paper. Some writers *need* this time off or they can't work at their best during their on periods.

The same applies to individual stories and poems. While sometimes I simply sit down and write pieces from beginning to end, there are also times when I feel the right thing to do is *stop* writing, put the piece aside for a while (a few days, a couple of weeks, even a few months), and come back to it later. This gives the piece, and the ideas and images therein, time to age and ferment in my mind.

Be willing to try a period of creative waiting when it feels appropriate—either for an individual piece or for all of your writing.

Putting a piece aside is also very useful when you feel that it's finished, or as close to finished as you can get it. If you put the story or poem away, forget about it for a while, and come back to it a week or a month later, you'll be able to read it with a fresh perspective. You should then be able to tell if it really *is* finished, or if it needs more work—and, if so, what sort of work it needs.

66

Stereotypes and Anti-Stereotypes

WE'VE ALL SEEN our share of stereotypes in literature and movies: the crooked lawyer, the timid accountant, the dim-witted Pole, the snooty Harvard graduate. We should also admit that stereotypes show up frequently in real life; there *are,* after all, some crooked lawyers, some timid accountants, and some snooty Harvard grads. But even the world's most timid accountant isn't *only* a timid accountant; he also has his own unique hopes, dreams, likes, dislikes, habits, fantasies, and so on.

The place of stereotypes in good writing is very limited. Stereotypes *have* been used successfully in some literary works (usually for comic effect); but this is rare, and you are best off avoiding stereotypes 98 percent of the time.

It is all too tempting to use stereotypes because they are much easier to create than characters that are living, breathing, full-fledged human beings. But this is precisely the reason to avoid stereotypes: they are convenient but second-rate replacements for art and for the sometimes difficult work of characterization.

The key to avoiding stereotypes is to show more than one—and preferably several—sides of a character's personality. This can often be done in a single image or detail, a single line of dialogue, or even a simple gesture, if you are careful and choose just the right item.

Each of us is unique. By showing your readers those details that make each of your characters different from everyone else (and especially from other members of their own ethnic, social, and professional groups), you transcend stereotyping and give your readers real human beings to read about. Don't let *any* of your characters be simply "a Jew," or "a college football player" or "a Swede" or "a lesbian." No one alive is that one-dimensional; why should your characters be?

This doesn't mean avoiding common traits of character or behavior. In the movie *Witness,* most of the characters were Amish, so it was necessary to give all of them Amish names, Amish accents, Amish clothing, and Amish customs. But several of the characters were full-fledged human beings instead of stereotypes because they were permitted to show actions and feelings *beyond* those all Amish hold in common.

Stereotypes are permissible in extremely minor characters—those called "spear-carriers" in dramatic works, because they do things like carry spears onstage and then leave. If you need to introduce an airline pilot just for one line, it's all right to show nothing more than a man or woman in a pilot's uniform. But if you are going to give your readers more than the briefest glimpse of a character, you must go beyond stereotyping.

Sometimes you can turn a stereotype around to positive effect. A good example here is Oliver Wendell Jones in the comic strip *Bloom County.* In many ways, Oliver is your typical computer nerd: he spends most of his day at his computer, wears thick glasses, has an enormous head, and often wears a white shirt and a narrow black tie. But Berke Breathed has avoided the stereotype by giving Oliver a sense of humor, by giving him some of the qualities of a normal small boy, and by making him black. (Our image of a computer nerd is almost invariably white.)

It is possible, however, to bend too far in the opposite

direction—to create characters who are exactly the *opposite* of their standard stereotypes. This technique can result, for example, in the female stevedore who lifts weights, loves watching TV football, and goes bowling with her girlfriends every Thursday night. Such a character is just as simplistic as a stereotype—indeed, it was created not through any act of skill, but simply by turning a stereotype on its head. This is simply another way of trying to avoid the work (and responsibility) of creating believable characters. The point is not merely to avoid stereotypes, but to avoid any approach to creating characters—or settings or situations—that relies on formulas rather than on craft and insight.

EXERCISE #18

WRITE A PIECE that takes place in a time other than our own, a culture other than our own, or both.

THINGS TO KEEP in mind:
- The culture may be mythical or imaginary if you wish. You may write about the gods of Ancient Greece, the people of Mu, Druids, aliens, dolphins, or even the lives of ghosts if you wish.
- "Another time" means before 1900 or after 2000. "Another culture" means a culture markedly different from the one westerners have lived in during this century.
- The piece must take place entirely within that other time and/or/culture.
- If you don't know enough about a culture or period to depict it accurately, feel free to fake it.

67

Pace

PACE, ALSO CALLED pacing or rate of revelation, is the speed at which events occur in a piece of writing. Pacing can refer to an entire piece; a particular scene or portion of a piece; or a single passage, description, or set of descriptions.

The basic technique of pace is simple: the more details you provide and the more words you use, the slower the pace. The more briefly you discuss or describe something, the faster the pace.

Here is the same incident described in three different ways, from the fastest pace to the slowest:

1) Frank took the bus downtown and got the money from his safe deposit box.

2) Frank waited forty minutes before the bus finally arrived. It took another twenty for it to lumber downtown, where the bank containing his safe deposit box was. At first the box wouldn't open, and Frank feared that the lock had been changed; then the key turned, and Frank carefully took all the money from the box and hid it in his money belt.

3) Frank chain-smoked cigarettes until his bus came. He had to wait forty minutes, and with each minute he became more anxious. When the bus finally arrived, it was packed with sweating secretaries and businesspeople on their way to work. Frank had to stand all the way downtown, and because of the rush-hour traffic the normally brief trip took

twenty minutes. When the bus finally reached his stop, Frank got off and walked slowly to his bank, doing his best to avoid attracting attention. One of the female tellers eyed him up and down as he entered; he couldn't tell whether she found him attractive or suspicious, or perhaps both. He made his way to the safe deposit boxes and fished in his pocket for the key. On his first three tries the lock would not turn, and for a frightening moment Frank thought, "They know all about the deal, and they've changed the lock on me." Then the key turned and the box slid out. As calmly as he could, Frank took the six thousand-dollar bills from the box and slid them inside his money belt.

Note that while the third example is the slowest-paced, it is also the most suspenseful and exciting. It is *not* always true that the faster the pace, the more exciting the scene or description. In fact, the fastest pace often occurs when nothing important is happening and you are simply trying to get your characters (and/or your reader) from one scene to the next. For example, imagine this line in a science fiction story: "Sandy spent that year traveling to Mars and back, as she had planned. But when she returned, Dan was no longer waiting." Then the story might go into detail about her reaction to this, at which point the pacing would slow way down.

A story or poem can be fast-paced in some sections, slow-paced in others, and in between in still others.

68

Series Pieces

ONE OF THE most interesting and inventive literary forms is the series piece.

A typical literary work takes a single general approach to a situation, predicament, setting, and/or group of characters. A series piece, however, is composed of three or more different but related sections, each of which takes its own unique approach or has its own particular perspective. Taken together, these multiple approaches or perspectives add up to more than the mere sum of their parts.

The series piece can adapt to every genre and to almost any literary style. It is by no means new (*The Thousand and One Nights* and *Canterbury Tales* are both series pieces), yet it remains as fresh and promising as ever.

Here are some other examples of series pieces:

● David Walker's group of poems "The Planets," in which each poem is about a different planet in our solar system.

● Lawrence Durrell's *Alexandria Quartet,* a group of four novels set in Alexandria, Egypt. All four novels recount the same events—but each book is from a different character's point of view.

● Crad Kilodney's "Office Worker's Dreams," a series of vignettes that all share office settings and an unsettling, eerie mood.

- John Steinbeck's *The Long Valley,* a collection of otherwise unrelated stories all set in California's Salinas Valley.
- John Donne's *Love Sonnets,* a group of sonnets all on the theme of love.

The series piece may be your ideal form when you have several different things to say about the same topic, when your ideas for a piece are going in several different directions at once, when you want to demonstrate multiple perspectives, or when a single approach to a piece simply isn't working.

A *series* piece should not be confused with a serial (also called a serialization), which is a single literary work published in two or more parts in successive issues of a magazine or newspaper.

EXERCISE #19

IF YOU HAVEN'T read chapter 68 yet, do so now.

Now, write a series piece of your own composed of several shorter pieces that share a common theme, image, character, location, or sequence of events—or some other common thread.

THINGS TO KEEP in mind:

• For a series piece to work well, it usually needs to be made up of at least three (and usually more) smaller pieces.

• Feel free to experiment with new or unusual ways to link all the smaller pieces together—for example, all the pieces might take place simultaneously, or all might include the same quote, or all might share the same minor but surprising element.

• Speaking generally, a successful series piece should be more than the mere sum of its parts. That is, the piece as a whole should say, do, or mean something that any of its parts taken alone does not.

IF NO IDEAS for a series piece come to mind, perhaps one of the ideas below will get you started:

• Think of a secret or special place you used to go to (or hide in) as a child. What were some of the things that happened to you there? What did you think or daydream about while you were there? What has become of that place now?

• What vice or virtue particularly angers or delights you? Think of some of the times when you saw this vice or virtue practiced, or when you practiced it yourself. Write down what happened. Make some of these items up if you wish. (One writer I know wrote an excellent story called "Lying" by simply recounting five anecdotes from her childhood; in each one, she told a lie, and that lie affected someone's life.)

• Think of an object that means a great deal to you—your bed, an item of jewelry, a stuffed bear, a certain book, a set of candlesticks. Make up several different anecdotes or stories about that object. Change the time, location, and/or characters from one anecdote to the next.

• Make a list of some of the things you most like to do. Pick one, and write several short pieces about the best, worst, most surprising, and strangest things that ever happened to you while you were engaged in this activity. Feel free to make things up.

69

Openings

YOU'LL RECALL FROM chapter 16 that you can begin a poem or story anywhere and in any manner you like. But that chapter talked only about the writing process, not about your finished pieces. Don't you need an opening line, sentence, image, or paragraph that will grab your reader?

Yes and no. Yes, you want to interest your reader. But no, you don't have to grab him by the neck and shake him.

Contrary to a fairly popular belief, your opening lines or sentences do *not* have to astound or shock your reader. You don't have to begin with a dead body, a knife fight, a cry for help, or a sex scene. You can give your readers more credit than this.

In fact, if you start out with a bang, you may simply dull your reader's senses. A knife fight isn't all that exciting if the reader doesn't know anything about who is in it or why it's happening. Furthermore, the sophisticated reader, seeing how hard you are straining to get his attention, may well be put off.

A student of mine once told me, "But my last writing teacher said I always had to start with the most exciting part." Not so. Should a murder mystery begin by revealing the name of the killer? Should a sex scene begin with orgasm? Of course not.

It is enough to simply begin at the beginning. You don't need any kind of zinger or special flourish. You don't need to write something that sounds or feels like an opening line. If your piece naturally begins with the image of children sledding down a hill, start right there, with no preliminaries.

Once your piece has reached the rewriting stage, look over its beginning. If it reads well as you've written it, leave it alone. Only if it feels unnatural or inappropriate should you tamper with it—and the point of your tampering should be to make it feel natural and appropriate, *not* to add some clever opening announcement, observation, or summary.

A good opening should fit naturally with the rest of your piece (or the rest of that section). It should lead the reader into the piece smoothly, without tricks or gimmicks.

Here's an example of a good opening for a prose piece: "I closed the window and took out my electric blanket; I knew I'd need it tonight, even though it was late June." This sentence leads the reader directly into the story by raising subliminal questions about the weather, the setting, the narrator's health and state of mind, and the events that will transpire later that night.

70

Endings

THE ADVICE ON openings in the previous chapter applies to endings as well. You don't have to have a snappy, hard-hitting, or thoroughly conclusive ending. You don't have to drive home a moral or make a point. (You can if you want to, however, provided you do it well.)

In fact, you don't need a special ending at all. Just as it is unnecessary and distracting to tack on an opening statement, it is counterproductive to add a final paragraph or stanza that adds a sense of closure. When the events have come to a stop, stop writing. You don't need to tack on a summary, a narrative conclusion, or a wrap-up. Your piece, if it has been written well, will likely provide its own natural conclusion.

Here are the kinds of things you should *not* add at the ends of pieces: "She realized then that the adoption would be impossible." "Someday he would return to the city; but for now, he was still just a country boy from Minnesota, and that suited him just fine." "It was her final message of hope—from beyond the grave." Each of these merely restates what the piece should have made abundantly clear by implication. (If a conclusion is *not* clear by implication from the rest of the piece, then it should be *made* clear through actions, details, images, and/or dialogue—not broadcast to the reader through a lecture or summary at the end.)

This all boils down to showing vs. telling (see chapter 40). Your piece should come to a conclusion that evolves naturally from its events, characters, and/or images. You don't have to tell the reader what the import or significance of the piece is; if you wrote it well, he or she already knows.

71

Titles and Names

A GOOD TITLE adds depth, meaning, nuance, emphasis, and/or perspective to a piece of writing; it does more than merely restate a theme or idea. It sets the tone of the piece and prepares the reader for it, at least subliminally.

Clever titles can catch readers' attentions. For example, the title *Stay Fit and Healthy Until You're Dead* is catchy, clever, and funny—and appropriate, because it clearly indicates that the book is a parody of exercise and health guides. *I Never Promised You a Rose Garden* is also catchy and appropriate, but in another way: its meaning and tone imply that the novel of that name will be about pain and adjustment. But clever and/or elaborate titles shouldn't be chosen for their own sake. Sometimes an understated title is more appropriate. Shirley Jackson's classic story "The Lottery" is perfectly titled: those two words, so flat and bland, prepare the reader beautifully for a story that begins with the commonplace, then builds slowly and inexorably to a peak of utter horror.

Dylan Thomas's story "The Peaches" is also flatly but aptly titled. In this case, the reader feels the impact of the title, which draws attention to a particular image and symbol in the piece, only *after* reading the story. When he rereads the title, he realizes how the peaches are representative of the differences between the two families in the story.

There are no rules to title-writing like "be jazzy" or "be straightforward and simple" or "make your reader curious." The only real rule is that a title must make a piece stronger, more meaningful, or more affecting.

Some writers write their titles first and their pieces second; some do it the other way around. Some come upon their titles while they're writing or rewriting. Do whatever works for you; this may differ from piece to piece.

And don't be too surprised if a publisher wants to change the title, even if you think it is perfect. A publisher looks at your work differently and may come up with an even better title.

AS FOR NAMES (of characters, imaginary places, corporations, or whatever), these generalities apply:

• Pick names that reflect the culture or subculture you're writing about. People in Chicago will have last names like Hwang, Morris, McWatt, Schwartz, Lund, Bogosian, Dean, Voivonich, Ondatu, and Hernandez. Don't give all your people from Chicago WASP names. Don't go to the other extreme, either, of making sure that all appropriate ethnicities are represented. This is just as artificial and inaccurate.

• Choose names that are reasonably interesting *and* reasonably easy to remember. Steinmetz is more interesting than Johnson. Tatercynzki is interesting, too, but too unfamiliar and complicated for readers to recall or pronounce easily. (You may, of course, use a difficult name if the very difficulty of that name is important to your piece.)

• Avoid names that may distract the reader. You want to keep your reader interested in your story or poem, not busy thinking about the strange name you came up with. Avoid names like Zitsling, Titlow, Ng, Drinkwater, and Butter. Names that sound or look humorous are especially to be avoided, unless you are specifically seeking a comic effect.

• Avoid stereotypes. Don't name a black man Leroy Johnson or a Jewish woman Ruth Goldblatt. Louis Witt and

Denise Katzman are more interesting and more three-dimensional.

• Make sure your reader can easily tell your characters' names apart. Don't put a Sue and a Suzanne in the same piece, or you'll confuse the reader as to which woman is which. (You may, of course, use both a Sue and a Suzanne to *cause* confusion, if such confusion is important to your piece.) Generally, even having a Sue and a Sandy can be a bit confusing because their names start with the same letter. Unless you have good reason to make two or more names similar, let them be recognizably different at first glance. Instead of Sue and Sandy, try Sue and Mandy.

• Don't telegraph messages through names. Don't call a timid woman Ms. Meek or a muscular, handsome man John Hero. Don't take the opposite tack, either (e.g., calling a Rambolike character Wendell Milk). Matching names and personalities is extremely annoying to intelligent readers.

• Don't try too hard to find names that are perfectly appropriate. After all, in real life names aren't chosen particularly well. A name that is believable, reasonably easy to remember, and not annoying or offensive will usually suffice. In fact, a name that is *too* appropriate may impress readers as artificial or unbelievable.

WITH RARE EXCEPTIONS, making final decisions on names and titles is part of the rewriting process. If you don't like a name or title you came up with, don't worry about it until you have finished writing and rewriting your piece. You can then fiddle with your title, and/or with your names, all you like.

EXERCISE #20

WRITE A PIECE that could have one of the following titles:

> "Around Here"
> "Going Under"
> "The Fourth Night"
> "Open Houses"
> "The World Inside"

THINGS TO KEEP in mind:
- If, as you write, you realize that your piece no longer fits well with any of the four titles above, don't try to force it to fit. Keep writing and forget the titles above.
- Once your piece is finished, if you can come up with a better title for it than one of the four listed above, use it.

Transitions

ONE OF THE most common, and most difficult, problems for new writers is transitions, the art of getting from one idea, image, setting, or situation to another.

This is usually much less of a problem than it seems. New writers tend to look for sophisticated or complicated solutions when simple ones will do very nicely. Here are some suggestions:

• Simply begin a new paragraph or stanza. This will often be all you need.

• In prose, skip a line and begin a new paragraph. This indicates a change of scene, setting, time, and/or point of view.

• Begin a new section or chapter.

• Begin a new paragraph or stanza and use a single transitional word or phrase (e.g., "Meanwhile . . . ," "The next morning . . . ," "When he arrived at the party . . .").

• Write a single short, crisp transitional sentence. Examples: "Suzy's office was not what Marlene had expected." "That weekend brought trouble." "When I saw his nephew, my fears were justified."

• Find a unifying image, concept, or word, then use it as a transition. There are *very* few things that are dissimilar in *all* ways. With a little thought and creativity, you can find something similar or related in almost any two images or situations. For example, suppose you need to get from an elderly woman eating an ice-cream cone to a cat sitting on top of a safe. You might write: "The way her tongue flicked at the ice cream reminded Todd of a cat lapping at milk. He thought of his own cat, Alexander, locked in the apartment alone. Todd knew Alexander would be sitting on the safe underneath the picture window, watching for Todd's return." Or: "The ice cream was melting slowly, and small drops were running down the side of the cone. Marilyn was suddenly aware of how hot it was outside. She longed to be back in her air-conditioned office drinking iced tea, her cat curled up next to her desk on the cool metal top of her safe."

● Fake it. *Make up* a unifying image concept, or word, then use it as an artificial bridge from one image or scene to the next. If you do it well, your reader will never notice that you've tricked him. Suppose you need to get from a dead rat to sixteen pennies on a tabletop. You might use the word "frozen" as your link: "The rat looked not so much dead as frozen solid—the way Jane's face had looked when he'd shown her the stolen coins the day before. 'All sixteen of them,' he had said as he spread them out on her dining room table. 'The only sixteen left in the world. Each one worth four thousand dollars.'"

Transitions are like beginnings and endings: new writers sometimes want to write specific transitional lines and paragraphs, when in fact their stories and poems naturally provide most or all of the transitions that are necessary.

As with other elements of good writing, transitions should be as simple, direct, and concise as possible.

ANOTHER COMMON WRITING problem is *uniting* two different or diverse scenes, ideas, themes, or images. Here again the problem is often more imaginary than real. The suggestions listed above can be used to unify diverse items as well as to provide transitions.

EXERCISE #21

WRITE A PIECE that begins with one of the following sentences or lines:

> I couldn't feel a thing.
> There are cars parked all over my lawn.
> It was him.
> No one I knew had ever seen him before.

THINGS TO KEEP in mind:
- You may replace "him" with "her" in either of the last two options above.
- If you prefer to use one of the above lines in the middle or end of a piece, rather than at the beginning, feel free to.
- If you'd like to make up your own opening line or sentence, go ahead.
- If none of the four lines does anything for you, try asking a friend to think of an intriguing (but not cutesy or gimmicky) sentence or line and write it down for you. Then use that line as the beginning of a piece. If you like, have your friend write several lines, or get one or two lines from each of several people. Then choose the line or sentence that most intrigues you.
- If more than one line gives you a good idea or image, go ahead and write each of them up if you wish.

73

Composite People, Settings, and Plots

ONE OF THE questions writers and writing teachers get asked most frequently is, "Where do you get your ideas?"

As you've figured out by now, we get them from everywhere: our own lives, the lives of people we know, reading and research, things we think up, our dreams and waking fantasies, our observations, and our meditations. You can put these together in any way you like to form what I call composite people, settings, and plots.

Suppose that in a story you want to create a character who is thoughtful and deliberate. You can, if you like, create this character largely or entirely from your imagination. But you can also think of some of the people you have met who intrigued you in some way. You might, for example, give this character the intense but bemused facial expression of your high school math teacher, the relaxed and steady gait of your aunt, and your oldest sister's habit of sticking to a single subject in a conversation until she's said everything she wants to on it. Keep in mind, however, that no one is *merely* thoughtful and deliberate. Each of us has thousands of different traits and attributes; some of these might even be contradictory. To make your character three-dimensional, you might want to give him your father's fondness for fast cars, your dentist's high-pitched giggle, and/or your boss's habit of scratching her nose when she feels nervous. You may even want to make this same character anything *but* deliberate about some things—for example, you might have him eat very quickly and greedily.)

Or suppose you want to create a cold, harsh hospital setting. You might combine the bright lights from the delivery room where you had your child, the worn and ugly furniture from a beauty salon you once went to, the dirty floor of a clinic you visited last year, and the grim, uninterested staff people you encountered at a hospital emergency room where you once went with a broken leg.

In short, vivid writing isn't just a matter of making things up; it's also a matter of recombining very real observations, experiences, and memories in new and moving ways. A composite character, for example, contains the traits of two or more different people, real and/or imaginary; a composite setting combines the details of two or more different places; and a composite plot or subplot combines the details of two or more different events.

74

The Karma Principle

KARMA IS A Sanskrit word that refers to the laws of cosmic cause and effect. According to the doctrine of karma, whatever actions you take today will in part determine what will happen to you in the future. For example, if you rob a bank, you will later suffer painful repercussions; even if you are never caught, you will undergo illness, injury, or deprivation. In comparison, those of us who do good deeds, according to the laws of karma, will have good fortune in the future.

This is not very different from Jesus' "as you sow, so shall you reap," or from the streetwise proverb, "what goes around comes around."

The concept of karma originated several millennia ago in India, and it is an important part of both the Buddhist and the Hindu religions. Modified slightly, it can be an extremely useful device for writing (and particularly for plotting) stories and poems.

What your characters say and do is naturally very important; but what happens *to* them can also be at least as important. In fiction and poetry, karma is the sense felt by the reader that certain people and circumstances have come together in just the right way. When events beyond a character's control combine with his or her plans, motivations, and decisions to advance the plot in a certain direction, a feeling of karma has been achieved. This sense of appropriateness can involve irony, timing, fate, and/or cosmic justice.

The simplest examples of karma occur in tales of adventure or suspense: the hero reaches the heroine seconds before the train runs over her; the detective discovers (either deliberately or by accident) the one clue that enables him to solve the mystery; James Bond defuses the bomb moments before it blows up half the Earth; the villain, who has trapped person after person, stumbles into his own trap.

More sophisticated literary works naturally require a more sophisticated use of the karma principle. For example, suppose a woman hurrying to catch a train sees something out of the corner of her eye. She almost passes by, but at the last moment turns to look at it. It is a small boy, lying unconscious under a bush. She revives the boy and locates his parents; when she reaches the train station, her train is already pulling out.

While she waits for the next one, she realizes that her husband will be very angry with her for being late. They are supposed to attend a wedding in two hours, and now they will be late for it. She is not good about being on time, and when she left her home that morning, her husband insisted that she take the six o'clock train back; she agreed and promised that nothing would make her miss that train. Now she has missed it. Nevertheless, she feels justified in missing it because the boy was clearly ill. At the same time she feels badly because her husband often criticizes her for putting the needs of strangers ahead of those of her family.

When she gets home, she finds her husband lying in the bedroom, unconscious, nearly dead, a knife in his chest. Many of their valuables are missing. She phones for an ambulance; her husband dies in it on the way to the hospital. Later the coroner tells her that the stabbing had likely occurred about forty minutes before she arrived; if she had caught the earlier train, she and her husband would have already left for the wedding by the time the robber entered their home.

If it were not for both the woman's kindness toward strangers and the particular circumstances that confronted her, her husband would still be alive. The woman now feels responsible for the death of her husband—the very person who tried to convince her that her kindness for strangers would result in more harm than good.

The biggest danger in employing the karma principle is in making things too obvious, too planned, too contrived. When this happens, the reader doesn't feel a sense of karma at all but, rather, the heavy-handed manipulations of the author.

Although you may deliberately employ the karma principle at any time, in many cases it will operate naturally in your work without any effort or planning on your part.

Word Choice

NO TWO WORDS are exactly alike. Even words that are often used interchangeably normally have slightly different shades of meaning, or at least different overtones or implications. At the very least, they have different appearances and sounds.

Take the words "pleased" and "happy." The two are considered more or less synonymous. But can you tell which of the faces below is pleased and which is happy?

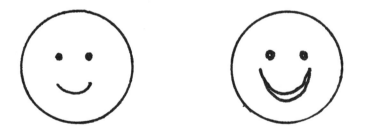

If you're like most people, you thought the face on the left is pleased and the one on the right is happy. Subconsciously, we consider happiness to be more intense than pleasure.

When it comes to words, the concept of "close enough" doesn't often apply. A word either means what you want it to mean, or it doesn't. Skipping is different from hopping. A huge piano is bigger than a large one. Musing is more meditative than speculating. An emaciated person is more than simply thin.

Distinctions such as these are particularly important in poetry and in prose poems, where each word carries a great deal of weight.

Many words have multiple and/or implied meanings. For example, the verb "mold" means "shape," but as a noun it also refers to a form of fungus associated with rot. If you are writing a poem about a funeral, you might choose the word "mold" over "shape" because of its subliminal reference to death. Or, if you are choosing between the words "cure" and "fix," you would choose "cure" for a more living, healthy effect, "fix" for a more mechanical, impersonal one. You might also choose to use a word ironically: if you wanted to show that your character was infatuated with his car, you might write that "he took the car to the mechanic, who healed its wounds."

Words differ in sound as well as meaning. "Clamber" means much the same thing as "climb," but it also *sounds* like someone climbing. "Car" sounds much more common-place and less stuffy than "automobile." A "family tree" sounds more personal and alive than a "geneology." And a "sofa" sounds softer and more yielding than a "couch."

Words also have meaning in the way they look on the page. The word "shriek" looks more strident than the word "scream." "Noggin" has a vaguely amusing appearance, even when it is used in a very serious sentence. A "dough-nut" looks more old-fashioned and handmade than a "donut."

Words subliminally imply other words with similar sounds, meanings, and appearances. "Motorcade" carries with it a subconscious image of a motor. "Breadth" subconsciously implies "bread." "Knows" implies "nose." "Steak" implies "stake."

In weighing one word against another, you will often find yourself considering two or more of the factors listed above (secondary meaning, sound, appearance, implications, etc.). Sometimes one word may be more appropriate in sound and appearance, but another may be closer in meaning. In such cases, consider what you gain and lose with each choice, and pick the word that produces the best overall effect. Reading pertinent passages aloud slowly and carefully with each possible variation will help you decide what word works best.

Usually it is best to let questions of word choice go until you have reached the polishing stage—or, in the case of some poems and prose poems, at least the revising stage. It's usually pointless to tinker with individual words earlier than this, as your piece hasn't yet really taken form.

Don't neglect the fine-tuning of word choice. Sloppily chosen or inaccurate words can blur the meaning of a line—in some cases even of a whole piece. And words that sound right and mean right can make that same piece a success.

76

How Much or Often Can I Break the Rules?

THIS QUESTION SOUNDS quite reasonable on the surface, but in most cases it's really rather irrelevant—like asking, "How much or often can I wear green?"

As a writer, whether or not you follow a particular rule isn't really an issue. What's important is that what you write be moving and absorbing. If you write good poetry or fiction that stays entirely within all rules and conventions, great. If your work ignores or breaks certain rules but is nevertheless successful, that's great, too.

Most of the best literary works follow conventions of form, grammar, spelling, and so on. But a good many do not. e. e. cummings, William Faulkner, Gertrude Stein, James Joyce, and a good many others built their careers, in part, by breaking conventions. Innovation is a vital and inevitable part of literature, and you can't have innovation without breaking rules. (The paradox of this, of course, is that the innovations of yesterday have become the conventions of today.)

In general, it is a good idea to follow the conventions of *language* (meaning, syntax, spelling, grammar, etc.) unless you have some reason to do otherwise. If you *do* have some good reason to break a rule or convention, however, go ahead and try it.

You can be more flexible still when it comes to form. The typical sonnet runs fourteen lines, but if you want to write a sonnetlike poem that runs sixteen lines, there's no reason on earth why you shouldn't. If a poem turns out well, what difference does it make whether it's a "proper" sonnet or not? Feel free to experiment with variations of established forms, and with entirely new forms and approaches. If something unorthodox seems promising, give it a shot.

Once that piece has been written, however, you need to ask yourself whether your approach worked. Innovation and experimentation are in themselves neither noble nor wicked; as one editor once said, "Experimentation is fine, but do we have to publish the failures?" If your piece turns out well, then your unorthodox approach is justified; if it doesn't, then you'll need to try another approach (perhaps a more standard one), or else file the piece away.

Is it all right to experiment just for the sake of experimentation? Sure. But the same standards apply to the finished product: if it's not good enough to show to an audience, don't try to publish it or read it before a group. (You may, of course, give it to friends, teachers, and/or critics for their reactions.)

One last word on this subject: some writers (and, unfortunately, a few writing teachers and editors) feel that most literary forms (e.g., the novel, the short story, and the villanelle) have very specific rules that *must* be adhered to. A simple survey of American literature proves these people resoundingly wrong: all our basic literary forms have been varied, redefined, and challenged, often by some of our best writers. You may stick to strict literary forms if you like—and many of our best contemporary writers still do—but you may also amend these forms or avoid them entirely, if you desire.

77

When Is a Piece of Writing Finished?

IT'S NOT ALWAYS easy to know when a story or poem needs no more rewriting or polishing. It's tempting to want to keep working on a piece, even when you think it's probably finished, to make sure you get it as close to perfect as possible. It's just as tempting to say "enough already" when the piece really does need more work.

These problems aren't unique to new writers. A lot of experienced writers have trouble knowing exactly when to stop.

Here are some general tips that should help:

• When a piece is done, it should sound right when read aloud and when read silently; it should look right on the page; it should "mean right"—that is, it should do what you want it to do, or have the effect you want it to have; and it should generally feel right to you.

• Follow your gut. If it tells you the piece is finished, it probably is. But if something about the piece still bothers you, even if you can't say why, the portion that bothers you probably needs more work.

• Don't let your eagerness to finish a piece alter your judgment. No matter how much you want your poem or story to be done, if it's not ready, it's not ready. If you're tired of working on the piece and it's still not done, put it aside and come back to it again later, when you're ready.

- Don't let perfectionism alter your judgment, either. Once you've gotten your piece in the best shape you can, don't keep going over and over it "to be sure."

- Some writers (myself included) often deliberately put pieces aside for a period of time after we feel we've finished them. For me it's usually a week or two; for other writers, the time varies from a couple of days to several months. Usually this time away from a piece enables us to approach it with a fresh perspective, and we can tell quickly whether or not it really is in final form.

- Some writers find they can tinker with their work indefinitely. If they followed this impulse faithfully, they'd never complete anything. If you find that you can go over and over a piece forever, keep working on it until the changes you are making are fairly minor; then *stop*. Resign yourself to never writing the perfect poem or story. Declare the piece finished, learn to live with its minor imperfections, and move on to another project. (This problem plagues quite a few published writers, who often complain to me that they are mortified when they see their work in print. To them, it looks unfinished and in desperate need of revision or editing; to their readers, it usually looks very good.)

- Watch for diminishing returns. As you near the end of the polishing phase, you'll likely find yourself making fewer and fewer corrections each time you go through the piece. Once you've gone through two times in which you made only a few minor changes, the piece is probably as finished as it's going to get. Declare it done.

- If you decide something is finished, you always have the option of changing your mind later on and working on it further.

78

How Do I Judge My Own Work?

THE THREE MAJOR questions you need to ask yourself in evaluating any piece of writing (including one of your own) are:

1) What is the piece trying to do? (This need not be easily explainable, or explainable in words at all.)
2) Does the piece do what it is trying to do or have the effect it is trying to have? How well does it succeed? Completely? Partially?
3) Is what it tries to do worth doing? (A serious story that demonstrates that bologna is a superior luncheon meat is not a story worth showing to others, and probably not a story worth writing.)

You can (and should) use these criteria to judge your own work. The better you get at judging others' work, the better you'll likely get at judging your own.

I sometimes get asked by my students, "Is it really possible for a writer to judge his or her own work objectively?" My answer is, "Of course. Can you tell when you've cooked an excellent omelet, when you've cooked a fair one, and when you've cooked a poor one?"

Naturally, some writers are better at making literary judgments than others. But the ability to make fair and legitimate judgments about literature (including your own work) is a skill that can be learned. The more you write, and the more you rewrite your own work, the better you are likely to become at making intelligent judgments.

Important: keep in mind that you are a beginning writer. Much or all of your work, at least for a while, is not likely to qualify as great literature, or even good literature—so don't expect it to. Your work will likely improve as you write more, but for the first few weeks or months, and possibly for the first year or two, your writing is still likely to be flawed and/or unsophisticated. There's nothing wrong with this at all, of course; *every* writer, alive or dead, started as a novice. Don't expect literary miracles from yourself.

Also remember that when you judge something you've written, you are judging only that particular piece—not your inherent or latent ability as a writer. To make a judgment *that* sweeping, you'll need to write at least several pieces over a period of some months. Don't make any snap judgments about your talent or your "career potential." It is tempting to make such judgments so that you can choose which direction(s) to pursue in the future—but a premature decision is often an incorrect one.

But what do you do if, after careful consideration, you realize that you've written something unsuccessful, or even downright awful? Either rewrite and polish it until it's in good shape, or file it away and move on to another project. Either way, don't waste any time or energy berating yourself—it's not necessary, appropriate, or helpful.

EXERCISE #22

LOOK BACK AT Exercise #4 and your response to it. You'll recall that for that exercise you wrote an account of a personal experience that was in some way painful for you.

Now, write a similar account—only this time you should tell the story of the single most frightening, most confusing, or most unbelievable thing that ever happened to you. As before, you should be truthful and accurate.

Also as before, tell your story in prose—not in poetry or drama. However, if, after you have written the prose version, you would like to write a poem or script based on that experience, or based on your prose account of that experience, go ahead.

THINGS TO KEEP in mind:
- Avoid saying or explaining how you felt. Instead, focus on what you did, said, saw, and heard (and smelled or tasted, if those senses are appropriate.)
- Tell your story as directly, as simply, and as straightforwardly as possible. Don't try to add any extra atmosphere or emotions, or any other embellishments. Avoid tricks or gimmicks. Simply show exactly what happened to you.
- If you wish, you may write the piece in the third person, with *he* or *she* as the subject instead of *I*. You may even make

up a character to be your protagonist if you like, but the story must still be a substantially true account of something that happened to you, and your character must behave much or entirely as you did in that situation.

Looking Back Once Again

BY NOW YOU'VE read most of this book and very likely done most of its exercises. Now is a good time to gather up everything you've written so far (including journal entries). Read it all through, then think about how far you've come, where you may be heading, and how you feel about it all.

Look back at chapter 35. Read through it, and ask yourself the questions in it once again. What do the answers to the questions tell you about the circumstances in which you write? About what you write? About what you want to write next? Can you see improvement in your work since you began writing? Since you last asked yourself these questions? Has your attitude toward writing changed at all?

Now we're ready to delve into the mechanics and techniques of the short story and the poem.

The Classic Short Story and Its Variations

THE MOST COMMON definition of the short story is also the most general: *any work of fiction shorter than novel or novella length.*

But there is also a much more specific definition that is used quite often: *a short story is a work of fiction shorter than a novel or novella in which one significant thing happens. One or more characters are beset by a problem; tension builds from that problem to a climax; change occurs, in one or in more characters and/or in their circumstances; a resolution of some sort is arrived at.*

This is the classical short story form. It makes use of plot, characters, conflict, tension, a climax, and a resolution. Most short stories, either by intention or by coincidence, follow this model.

Some writing teachers feel this model is the *only* acceptable one, and teach it as such; but literature has given us hundreds of successful stories that are structured very differently. Some writers who have built entire careers writing nontraditional short stories include Richard Brautigan, Robert Coover, Jorge Luis Borges, and Donald Barthelme.

While you are welcome to write a story that very deliberately conforms to the standard short story model, you are just as free to use alternative models (see below) or no models at all. If you like, make up your own form, structure, or approach to suit the needs of your particular piece.

Actually, fiction writers rarely choose a form first and then write a piece to fit it. (This approach is much more common in poetry, where there are many specific forms to choose from, such as sonnets, villanelles, haiku, etc.) Much more often, fiction writers simply say what they need to say and let the content of the piece naturally determine its form.

HERE ARE SOME alternate models for short stories that have been used successfully:

- The vignette or slice of life. This is a sort of still-life with characters. Characters and situations are rendered sharply and clearly, but there is normally no climax or resolution, and sometimes little or no conflict. The purpose of a vignette is to simply immerse the reader in a particular setting and/or situation.
- The series story. See chapter 68 for a discussion of these pieces.
- The cubist story. This form was developed in the 1960s by Robert Coover, who has used it repeatedly. A cubist story begins with a few central characters, images, and themes; these are then combined over and over, in different ways, in a series of brief sections, each of which depicts a single incident. Some of the sections may partially overlap others; some may contradict others. The effect is much like that of a cubist painting, in which many views and variations of the same image are seen simultaneously. The most successful and popular cubist story is Robert Coover's "The Babysitter." Other writers have written stories in this form as well.
- The fictional essay. An imaginary memoir, biography, diary, book review, press release, etc. Jorge Luis Borges (who, rather than write certain novels, would write reviews of them) is the contemporary master of this form. Woody Allen has also done much with the fictional essay. Some of the most unusual examples of this form include epistolary

pieces, which are made up of fictional correspondence; stories written in the form of multiple-choice tests; pieces that are made up of news reports, TV and radio broadcasts, and other fictional excerpts from the media; and a piece in the form of listings in *TV Guide.*

- The prose poem. See chapter 50 for a definition.

EVERY STORY, REGARDLESS of its form, contains the following elements:

- Plot (what happens, how it happens, and why it happens)
- Setting (where it happens)
- Time (when it happens)
- Characters (who it happens to)

You may begin your story with any one (or combination) of these elements—or with a quote; an idea; a theme; an image; or a word, phrase, or sound that intrigues you.

A short story can be any length—or, rather, it should be as long or as short as it needs to be. If what starts out as a short story turns into a novel or a prose poem, that's fine. Duane Ackerson has published an excellent short story called "Sign at the End of the Universe," which is three words long. It has, by implication, all the elements listed above, and in its three words it makes a statement about our existence that is both wise and funny.

81

Talking with Your Characters

SOMETIMES CHARACTERS SEEM to create themselves out of nothing; sometimes they defy their creators and do things they're not supposed to do.

If you want one of your characters to act a certain way, and he or she refuses to or is unable to, don't force the issue. Instead, let that character do what he or she seems to want to do. Just keep writing. If you have no idea what the character has in mind or why he or she is behaving so strangely, *still* just keep writing and see what happens. Sometimes characters know better than their creators what to do next or where their story should go.

One excellent technique for simultaneously creating and getting to know a character is to have a chat with him or her. Place two chairs facing each other, a few feet apart. (You may do this mentally if you like; but some writers find it helps to set up two real chairs.) Sit in one and imagine your character in the other. How is he dressed? How is he sitting—bolt upright, slouched, legs crossed, hands in his lap? Is he relaxed or nervous? What movements, if any, is he making?

Now ask him some questions, either silently or out loud. (Some writers find that actually speaking produces better results.) Then listen for his answer. Don't try to imagine what he would or should say; instead, relax and listen to what pops into your head. Ask questions for as long as you like, or until you get the answers you need. If you like, write down those answers.

You can do this at any stage (or even every stage) of the writing, rewriting, and polishing processes, and you can of course ask any questions you wish. In some cases you might interview a character before you start writing; in others you might call a character in for an interview when you're stuck and don't know where to go next; in others, you might ask a character for a particular response. (For example, "Okay, Colette, you're stuck in the back of the store with this angry stranger. What do you do?")

Here are some variations on this technique that some authors have used successfully:

• Bring two or more characters together, and get a conversation going between them.

• If you want to know how a character handles, say, being complimented, say to him, "You look great today," and see what he says and does in response. Look for gestures and small mannerisms, and listen for inflections.

• Ask a character to interview *you.*See what he does, what questions he asks, etc.

• Instead of just listening for a character's answer in your head, let him speak out loud, using your mouth. If you like, use your character's inflections, accent, and manner of speaking. You can take this one step further and sit in the character's chair when he or she is talking.

Rather than simply staging a conversation, some writers sit back and imagine that an entire scene is playing itself out before them. Try this out yourself, with your eyes either open or closed, as you prefer. Create an imaginary setting and situation; then bring in the appropriate characters, and let them loose. Passively watch what they do, and what happens to them, and write it all down.

Talking with characters will seem a bit odd at first, but after you've done it a couple of times it will seem extremely normal. However, it is very wise to let the people you live with know in advance exactly what you are doing; an uninformed observer might wonder about your sanity.

82

Anyone Can Understand Good Poetry

POETRY IS WRITTEN in English. There is no special secret to reading and understanding it; nor do you need any special training to be able to follow and enjoy it.

Yet intelligent, literate people often tell me, "I don't understand poetry"—and even, "I *can't* understand poetry."

When I hear comments like these, my response is usually, "Do you have trouble with Robert Frost's poems?" The answer is always, "no." Then I ask, "Do you enjoy his work?" So far the answer has been "yes" every time. But often people have added, "But that's not really *poetry*, is it?" At this point I laugh, because Frost is widely (and properly) recognized as one of the greatest American poets of the century.

So why do people think his work isn't poetry at all? Simple: *because they can understand it.*

There exists on this continent a myth that poetry is too highbrow or complicated for ordinary people to understand; that it is written in some language other than English that only critics, literature professors, college students, and other poets can follow; that it is inevitably serious and never fun; and that it *should* be all these things. If it isn't, it must not be poetry at all.

A simplified version of this myth goes like this: poetry is not meant to be understood by normal people (or by anyone at all). If I understand it, it must not be very good; if it confuses me, it's probably brilliant.

I have run into this myth time and time again. I don't just hear it from people I meet on the street; I hear it from friends, from my own writing students, and even from college professors (though never, of course, from English professors).

Yet everything about this myth is completely false—as thoroughly and obviously false as the statement, "All poets are from Ohio." So where in the world does this myth come from, and why is it so persistent and pervasive?

Part of the blame goes to English teachers, who often (unwittingly) teach students that poetry cannot be understood without their insights and explanations; part goes to poetry publishers, who design poetry books that physically *look* highbrow and inaccessible; and part goes to poets themselves, who sometimes act as if they're bursting with high culture and lofty thoughts.

The myth is further perpetuated by the fact that in North America the writing, publishing, and public performance of poetry are intimately connected with academia. Most major poetry magazines and books are published by university presses; most poetry readings are held on college campuses; and most well-known poets teach poetry writing at colleges and universities.

Another reason why the myth of inaccessibility persists is that rarely are people willing to say, "This poem isn't very good." The fact is that most contemporary poetry *isn't* very good, for the simple reason that most of what gets published in *any* genre isn't very good. (For more details on this observation, see chapter 90.) But although most of us are willing to say "that was a boring story" or "that was a dumb movie," many of us, when confronted by a bad poem, will say, "I don't understand this" rather than "What an awful piece of poetry!"

Why the fear of stating an honest opinion? Why do so many people consider poetry immune to criticism? Why do they think that if a poem isn't successful, the fault must be in the reader, not in the poem?

I suspect that many readers, all too aware of the close ties between poetry and academia, feel (albeit subconsciously) that to say anything bad about a particular poem is to criticize our whole academic and intellectual heritage. But a poem can (and should) be criticized separately from the intellectual tradition from which it springs, just as a story, play, song, movie, TV show, or novel can.

People are also afraid to criticize poetry because they fear that if they do, they'll be attacked—or at least sneered at—by professors, critics, English majors, and/or other literary types. Most of all, they're afraid of being thought of as dumb or uncultured.

But to be able to enjoy writing—or even reading—poetry at all, you need to be able to say about a particular poem, "I don't like this." And you have every right to say this, either about something you've read in a book or magazine, or about something you've written yourself. Until you give yourself the freedom to dislike a poem (no matter what other people may say or think about it), you'll have no way to judge how well *any* poem works, including one you've turned out yourself.

None of this is to say that all poetry should be written in the style of Robert Frost. Poetry encompasses an extremely wide range of styles. Nor am I implying that poetry must be logically and immediately understandable to be enjoyed. There are some excellent poems that need to be read several times before their intentions become clear; there are successful poems that involve complex language and imagery and that need to be read quite carefully; there are successful poems that aren't logical at all and that rely primarily on associations of image, symbol, and/or metaphor; and there are good poems that are downright surrealistic.

But what if you genuinely *can't* understand a poem, either with your mind or with your gut? Read it again, carefully. If it's no clearer or more moving, chances are it's not a very good poem.

Incidentally, the myth that poetry is a highbrow art form, and that it must be confusing to be good, isn't quite as pervasive as it may seem. The myth is widely accepted in North America, but in many other countries—France and Ireland, for example—poetry is regarded as neither highbrow nor special. In these countries, people (including "common people") read poetry regularly for pleasure.

83

Daffodils, Gibberish, and Nestor: The Most Common Mistakes in Poetry

ALL OF US are exposed to bad poetry every day—in greeting cards, newspaper ads, TV and radio jingles, popular songs, and other forms of mass-market culture. Most such poetry is simplistic, poorly written, overexcited, and cliched.

Because this kind of poetry is all around us, some new writers try to copy its forms and approaches. These writers turn out poems that begin with lines like "Love is like a rose" and "Spring is in the air." "Inspirational" poems are especially common.

There's nothing wrong with writing inspirational poems, or poems about love, roses, spring, or anything else. There *is* something wrong with using cliches and rotten poems as models for your own work, because your own poems are almost certainly going to turn out just as poorly. If you are seeking some models, you are much better off looking to a good poetry anthology, such as *The Norton Anthology of Poetry*.

Other new writers take a different tack: they string together a group of grand-sounding phrases and/or interesting images, in the mistaken belief that this will create a good poem. But a poem must be more than a collection of nifty or interesting stuff; it must hold together in an organized (though not necessarily logical or symmetric) fashion.

A variation on this theme is the poem that is *deliberately* obscure or confusing. A few new writers subscribe to the myth that good poetry *should* be confusing; or they mistakenly believe that poems should be puzzles that the reader is obliged to figure out. These writers sometimes think that this obscurity expresses depth, cleverness, intelligence, or sophistication; in fact, it expresses their ignorance. (A good rule of thumb: any poem—or any piece of writing—that tries to impress you with its author's cleverness, wisdom, or ability is probably not a very good piece.)

Another variation is the poem loaded with literary or intellectual allusions—usually to philosophers, artists, Ancient Greeks, and/or other writers. There's nothing wrong with making allusions in a poem, or in any piece of writing; but there should be a good reason for doing so. Merely mentioning—or, worse, listing—names isn't going to do a thing for your poetry, no matter how revered the people bearing those names may be. A few writers use these allusions to demonstrate how knowledgeable or well-read they are; what they actually prove, of course, is that they are egotists who mistake flaunting their knowledge for good poetry.

Rhymed vs. Unrhymed Poetry

WHICH IS BETTER: rhymed or unrhymed verse? Neither, of course. Each poem, whether it rhymes or not, must be judged on its own merits.

Which is more difficult to write? It depends on the individual writer and the particular poem. Rhymed poetry, particularly such forms as the sonnet and the villanelle, provides an established structure to work within. For some writers, this structure provides guidance and useful limits; for others, it inhibits rather than encourages creativity.

Which is more contemporary? Neither. Some people think that rhymed poetry has gone out of style. This is utterly untrue. Both rhymed and unrhymed verse continue to appear in literary journals, including some of the most popular and prestigious ones. It *is* true that nowadays *most* published poetry does not rhyme and that a century ago most published poetry did. However, there has never been a period of literary history in which *only* rhymed or unrhymed verse was considered legitimate. Both the rhymed and the unrhymed poem have been around for many centuries.

Which should you write? Either one, or both, as you please.

Poetic Terms and Techniques

HERE IS A short dictionary of terms commonly used in writing, critiquing, and discussing poetry. *It is not necessary to memorize or use these terms to write good poetry*. This dictionary is provided primarily for reference purposes.

STANZAS

Every poem is composed of one or more STANZAS, or groups of lines. Where each line ends is called a LINE-BREAK; where each stanza ends is a STANZA-BREAK. Where lines and stanzas begin and end is important; line-breaks and stanza-breaks add a slight visual (but not aural) accent and pause.

In sophisticated poetry, sound and appearance often have separate effects. For example, sentences and phrases do not always end where the lines and stanzas do.

Poetry should normally be read according to sentence structure, *not* according to the structure of lines and stanzas; in general, when reading poetry aloud, you should not pause at the end of a line unless a punctuation mark indicating a pause appears.

When one line leads directly into the next without a pause, this is known as ENJAMBMENT or RUN-ON LINES; such lines are said to be ENJAMBED. When a pause is intended at the end of a line, this line has an END-STOP, and is said to be END-STOPPED. A pause *within* a line is called a CAESURA.

Stanzas can be as short as a single line (or even a single word) or as long as an entire poem. The following terms are used for the most common stanza-lengths:

COUPLET: two-line stanza.
TERCET or TRIPLET: three-line stanza.
QUATRAIN: four-line stanza.
CINQUAIN or QUINTET: five-line stanza.
SEXTET or SESTET: six-line stanza.
SEPTET: seven-line stanza.
OCTAVE: eight-line stanza.

SOUND DEVICES

Nearly everything in a poem is a sound device of some sort; rhyme and metrics (see below) constitute distinct categories of sound devices.

Below are some sound devices common to all poems, rhymed and unrhymed, metrical and nonmetrical:

Alliteration
Similar initial sounds in two or more words, e.g., sad sack, green grasslands, frightening phantasm. The phrase "pale phantasm" is *not* alliterative.

Assonance
Similar vowel sounds, e.g., rat trap, hated neighbors, high-minded writer.

Consonance
Similar consonant sounds, e.g., ostentatious stamp, redundant document, dark corner.

Onomatopoeia
Words and phrases that sound like the objects or actions they describe, e.g., gulp, hiss, nerd, croak, growl, etc.

RHYME

Rhyme (or true rhyme)
Rhyme refers to two or more words with identical sounds in their final vowels; if these words end in one or more consonants, the sounds produced by these consonants must also be identical. Examples: spit and hit, connect and direct, shoe and flew, spittoon and bassoon, time and rhyme, miniature and photogravure. Also called MASCULINE RHYME or SINGLE RHYME—as opposed to FEMININE RHYME or DOUBLE RHYME (see below).

Double rhyme (or feminine rhyme)
These refer to words and phrases with identical final syllables and with *next-to-last* syllables that rhyme, e.g., fountain and mountain, hero and zero, surrender and pretender, down by the bayou and out in Ohio. TRIPLE RHYMES (which are also considered feminine rhymes) occur when the last *two* syllables of each word are identical and rhyme occurs in the prior syllable. Examples: Victorian and de Lorean, terrarium and aquarium, clarity and polarity.

Slant-rhyme
Entails identical final vowel sounds *or* identical final con-

sonant sounds, but not both. Examples: blame and stain, courageous and Caracas, bell and sail, worst and best, ice and prize, beaten and season, surrender and asunder. Slant-rhyme is also known as NEAR-RHYME, IMPERFECT RHYME, OFF-RHYME, and HALF-RHYME.

Eye rhyme
Words that rhyme in the way they look, but not in the way they sound, e.g., pain and again, pie and brie, sight and freight.

Internal rhyme
Rhyme that occurs within a single line of poetry, e.g., "My body aches from past mistakes."

Rhyme scheme
A pattern of rhyme in a poem. In a quatrain in which lines one and three rhyme with each other and lines two and four rhyme with each other, the rhyme scheme is written *abab*. If all four lines rhyme with one another, the rhyme scheme is written *aaaa*. If only the second and fourth lines rhyme, the rhyme scheme is *abcb*.

METRICS

Metrics (or meter)
Refers to a pattern of stressed and unstressed (also called accented and unaccented) syllables within a line. In the word "window," the first syllable is stressed and the second unstressed; in the word "casino," the second syllable is stressed and the first and third unstressed. A stressed sylla-ble is also called an ACCENT.

243

Not all poems have regular meter, though rhymed poems often do. Some poems have meter but no rhyme; in others, the meter changes from stanza to stanza or line to line.

A group of two or three syllables is called a POETIC FOOT. A single foot may consist of one, two, or three words, or of only a portion of one word.

There are seven basic poetic feet. Each is made up of a different arrangement of stressed and unstressed syllables. These seven feet, and examples of each, are listed below:

IAMB (or IAMBIC FOOT): renew, goodbye, go home, surprise.

TROCHEE (or TROCHAIC FOOT): hangnail, doorknob, soup bowl, eggnog.

DACTYL (or DACTYLIC FOOT): Saturday, herringbone, angel food, speak to me.

ANAPEST (or ANAPESTIC FOOT): resurrect, overdrawn, open mind, cigarette.

AMPHIBRACH (or AMPHIBRACHIC FOOT): courageous, surrender, tremendous, the palace.

SPONDEE (or SPONDAIC FOOT): two equally stressed syllables in a row. Examples: no way, White House, heartburn, big top, wigwam.

PYRRHIC (or PYRRHIC FOOT): two unstressed syllables in a row. Examples: in a, with the, so she.

Long words may contain two or more feet. The word "overwhelming" is made up of one pyrrhic and one trochee.

It is possible for words and phrases to be pronounced (and read) in more than one way. For example, the phrase "going crazy" can be read as two trochees or as a pyrrhic and a trochee. The word "fire" can be read as one syllable or two.

Feet that end on a stressed syllable are said to have RISING METER; those that end on an unstressed syllable have FALLING METER.

A line that consists of a single foot is a line of MONOMETER. A line that consists of the same type of foot repeated twice (with no other syllables before, after, or in between) is DIME-TER; a line consisting solely of the same type of foot repeated three times is TRIMETER; four times, TETRAMETER; five times, PENTAMETER; six times, HEXAMETER; seven times, HEPTAM-ETER.

The meter of a poem is based on the kind and number of feet in each line. A poem in which each line contains six trochees is written in TROCHAIC HEXAMETER. Sonnets have fourteen lines of five iambs each, so they are written in IAMBIC PENTAMETER.

It is perfectly fine to use several different kinds of poetic feet in the same line. This is known as MIXED METER.

To SCAN a poem is to identify the type and number of feet in each line. How a poem scans is called SCANSION.

MISCELLANEOUS TERMS

Alexandrine
Any twelve-syllable line.

Blank Verse
Unrhymed iambic pentameter. Blank verse is very different from free verse (see below).

Canto
A section of a poem. Cantos are often numbered and usually (though not necessarily) consist of several, or many, stanzas. A canto is to a poem what a chapter is to a novel.

Free Verse
Verse written without meter or regular rhyme. Free verse can (and should) make use of other poetic techniques. You'll

recall from chapter 56 that free verse has nothing in common with either automatic writing or stream of consciousness.

Lyrical
Synonymous with the adjective "musical." A lyrical poem is one with especially strong rhythm and sound devices. Not to be confused with a LYRIC POEM, which is a short poem that expresses a single emotion, narrated by a single speaker.

Prosody
The study of formal patterns of sound, such as meter and rhyme.

Refrain
A phrase, line, group of lines, or stanza that appears repeatedly in a poem, sometimes with alterations or variations.

Sonics
How a poem sounds; the combination of rhyme, meter, and sound devices. I have heard the word PHONICS used synonymously.

THIS CHAPTER HAS defined and described a wide variety of poetic techniques. While you may, if you like, deliberately use some of these techniques in your writing, this is not the way most poetry gets written. You'll find, instead, that you'll use many of these poetic techniques naturally, without making a conscious effort to employ them. You'll write some words or lines that sound and feel right; only later will you realize that you've made use of, say, assonance, onomatopoeia, and internal rhyme.

Readers interested in studying poetic devices and forms in more depth should look at Paul Fussell's *Poetic Meter and Poetic Form* (Random House).

86

Tips for Writing Poetry

HERE ARE SOME brief but useful suggestions for writing poetry:

- Poetry should be as concise, as simple, and as clear as possible, while still doing everything you want it to do.
- Get your reader to use his or her senses. Show him images, actions, and events that are clear, specific, and concrete.
- A poem can tell a story. A great many poems throughout history, in fact, have told stories, from Homer's *Iliad* and *Odyssey* to "Casey at the Bat" to "The Death of the Hired Hand." A poem doesn't *have* to tell a story, however.
- Most good poetry emphasizes sound as well as imagery. How poetry sounds is often as important, or nearly as important, as what it says or means. Indeed, in good poetry sound becomes part of the meaning.
- A poem should be as long as it needs to be—no shorter or longer. A poem may be as long as a book; in fact, two book-length poems (which might also be called novels in verse), Marilyn Hacker's *Love, Death and the Changing of Seasons* (Arbor House) and Vikram Seth's *The Golden Gate* (Random House) were published not too long ago.
- Successful poems have also been very short. Ezra Pound and Charles Wright have both written well-received two-line poems. A poem can be still shorter: a single line, or even a

single word. When I serve as writer-in-residence in public schools, I often ask my students to write one-line and one-word poems; every class produces at least a few good ones.

• To write good free verse, you must pay as much attention to structure, rhythm, line-breaks, stanza-breaks, and other poetic devices as you would in writing more rigidly structured poems. Free verse implies freedom from a specific structure; it does *not* mean you needn't employ poetic technique.

• Strenuously avoid—or catch and eliminate—all cliches. Keep in mind that an image can be just as cliched as a word or a phrase. The organ grinder with the monkey in a little red coat, the hog wallowing in mud, and the mustached painter with a beret are all overused, cliched images.

• Now is an excellent time to reread chapters 37-40. These chapters apply at least as much to poetry as they do to fiction.

87

Forms of Poetry

I SAID EARLIER that, in general, the form of a poem or story should be determined by what that piece says or does. Most contemporary verse follows this principle.

However, you do have the option of writing poems that follow a specific, standardized form. A number of such literary forms have developed over the centuries, and all have been widely used. Here are the most common ones:

Ballade
A poem normally composed of three eight-line stanzas, each rhyming *ababbcbc,* followed by a four-line stanza that rhymes *bcbc.* Not to be confused with a BALLAD, which is a poem or song that tells a story and that usually (though not necessarily) rhymes *abcb* or *abab.*

Haiku
A seventeen-syllable poem of three lines. Lines one and three are five syllables each; line two is seven syllables. The haiku originated in China and Japan; the word "haiku" is Japanese. Traditionally, a haiku contained a single image, observation, or setting, almost always involving some aspect of

nature. Haiku written in English employ the traditional three-line, seventeen-syllable form, but not necessarily the naturalistic, single-image approach.

Rondel

A fourteen-line poem that rhymes *abbaabababbaab*. Lines seven and eight repeat the first two lines, as do lines thirteen and fourteen.

Sestina

A poem of six six-line stanzas followed by one three-line stanza. In each stanza after the first, the final words of lines one, two, three, four, five, and six are the same as the final words of lines six, one, five, two, four, and three of the previous stanza. The final three-line stanza incorporates all six of these words. Sestinas normally do not rhyme.

Sonnet

A fourteen-line poem, usually in iambic pentameter. A variety of rhyme schemes have been used, but the three most common are *abbaabbacdecde, abbaabbacdcdcd,* and *ababcdcdefefgg*. Edmund Spenser employed the variation *ababbcbccdcdee*.

Villanelle

A poem made up of five three-line stanzas, each rhyming *aba,* and a final four-line stanza, often (though not necessarily) rhyming *abaa*. Lines six, twelve, and eighteen repeat line one; lines nine, fifteen, and nineteen repeat line three.

IN ALL THE rhyming poems except the sonnet, the choice of metrics is up to the author—though normally *some* metrical system (e.g., iambic tetrameter), rather than mixed meter, must be employed. One line cannot be two syllables and the next one eighteen. (This principle, by the way, does not apply to free verse.)

Poems employing all of these forms can be found in poetry anthologies. With the exception of ballades and rondels, all of these forms are still used and published today.

Keep in mind that you don't have to follow any of these forms strictly. Many successful poems bend the rules of their forms slightly. Other good poems are deliberate variations of traditional forms. Feel free to experiment.

EXERCISE #23

WRITE A PIECE about a black box, or involving a black box.

THINGS TO KEEP in mind:
- The black box can be any size or shape.
- The box can be anything real or imaginary.
- What is inside the box—if there is anything in it at all—may or may not be important, and may or may not be revealed.
- If you prefer, write about a silver box, or a black hole, instead.

88

A Writer's Library

THERE ARE HUNDREDS of books available on every possible writing topic, as well as on writing in general. These books naturally range in quality from wonderful to awful. Only a very few books, however, can genuinely be considered necessities for writers.

The most essential book for writers is a good, thick dictionary—the bigger the better. An unabridged one is best. If you don't want to spend a lot of money, get the thickest paperback dictionary you can easily find. Because meanings of words are constantly changing, and because new words and usages are being added to our language all the time, it is a good idea to own an up-to-date dictionary—one no more than five years old.

The next most essential reference book for writers is a thesaurus. This is a book that lists synonyms, words that have similar meanings. When I look up the word "sofa" in my dictionary, here is what I get: "A long upholstered seat or couch, usually with a back and raised ends or arms." But when I look up the same word in my thesaurus, I get this: "settee, davenport, couch." As with dictionaries, the bigger the thesaurus the better. (There is no such thing as an "unabridged" thesaurus, however.) Get a thesaurus that lists words alphabetically, rather than by general topic;

alphabetical ones are much easier to use. A variety of paperback versions are available at low cost.

The one other basic book that can benefit nearly every writer is *The Elements of Style* by William Strunk and E. B. White (Macmillan). This is the best, briefest, most concise, most readable, most down-to-earth, and most useful manual of style and usage available. It can be read enjoyably from cover to cover, but its primary use is as a reference guide to clear and interesting writing and to proper English usage.

If you are a poor or mediocre speller, you should also purchase a dictionary of commonly misspelled words, listed alphabetically by their proper spellings. Paperback versions (usually with titles like *1001 Misspelled Words*) are available. I also recommend *The Bad Speller's Dictionary* (Random House), which lists commonly misspelled words alphabetically by their most common *incorrect* spellings. Correct spellings appear next to the misspellings.

Keep these reference books handy so that you can use them easily whenever you need to. If you have a large dictionary that's difficult to lift, keep it on a table or dictionary stand. Most important, *use* these books! The best reference book in the world is worth nothing if you never refer to it.

Other recommended books on more specific writing topics are noted in chapters 95-98.

89

"I Can Write Better Than That": Why So Much Trash Gets Published

ALL OF US have read published poems, stories, articles, and books that we thought were poorly written or conceived. The natural reaction to reading these pieces is, "If this is all the writing talent it takes to be published, then I ought to be able to make millions as a writer. I can write at least as well as this."

It is of course possible that you've missed the piece's intent or approach, or that it was butchered through improper editing. But in many cases your comment will be right on target: the piece *won't* be very good.

The simple fact is that most of what gets published in every field of writing isn't very good. But before you come up with a theory to explain this phenomenon, be assured that *throughout history* most of what has been published hasn't been very good.

Poor writing seems more common these days for two reasons. First, more material is simply being published now than ever before. Second, the vast majority of badly done literary works written more than a few years ago have disappeared. As the years pass, mediocre and poor writing tends to vanish into obscurity, while the best material tends to survive. (There are some exceptions: good material disappears also, and a few insufferable works have managed to become "classics." But in general the point holds.) But time has not had a chance to weed out the awful and mediocre works published in the last few years.

There's another, more important, reason why many poor pieces of writing get published, and this one is economic. In free-market countries like the United States, Canada, the United Kingdom, and Australia, the great majority of publishers are in business primarily to make money. Most publishers, then, tend to publish what people will most be willing to buy—or at least what they believe people will most be willing to buy. The ghostwritten autobiography of a soap opera star will almost inevitably sell *two hundred times* as many copies as a book of poems by a new poet—even if the autobiography is badly written and the book of poems a literary masterpiece. If you wanted to make a living as a publisher, which would you publish?

This doesn't mean you should write trash or that you should write for the largest possible audience. You should continue to write for whatever audience suits you (including "the masses," if you like), no matter how large or small it may be. Just don't have any illusions that your new book of villanelles will hit the bestseller list or that your wildly experimental short story about Socrates will be published by *Redbook.*

90

The Publishing Establishments

TWO VERY DIFFERENT kinds of publishing exist side by side in North America (and in most countries): commercial publishing and literary publishing. Commercial publishers are in business primarily (and in some cases solely) to make a profit; literary publishers, on the other hand, are more concerned with publishing good work simply because it *is* good. In general, commercial magazines, newspapers, and books reach tens of thousands to millions of people; literary publications reach a few hundred to a few thousand. (These figures are for the United States and Canada.) There is a lot of money to be made in commercial publishing; with some exceptions, there is more prestige and a great deal less money in literary publishing.

Each publisher naturally has its own preferences and makes its own choices; but some general differences between literary and commercial publishing can be described.

Commercial publishers are usually interested in accessibility, readability, and popular themes. Plot and ideas are usually more important than style or imagery, though an author's reputation is often more important than all four. Unusual or experimental forms, approaches, or themes are discouraged. Some commercial publishers (publishers of romance, mysteries, adventure fiction, westerns, generational sagas, and most men's and women's magazines) expect their writers to follow specific formulas in their pieces.

Commercial fiction and poetry reflect current fashions and trends and usually uphold the status quo. Such work is intended to comfort rather than challenge, confront, or jar its readers. Poetry in commercial publications is often sentimental, overdramatic, or silly. Commercial publishers almost never publish surrealism, allegory, vignettes, prose poems, or rhyming poetry longer than twenty lines.

Literary publishers are open to a wider range of material. They do not respond to *popular* fashions or trends, but they do follow separate literary ones (which are arbitrary and subject to change). They are generally interested in sophisticated stories and poems; however, they will occasionally publish well-written mysteries, horror pieces, or works of science fiction or fantasy. Literary publications occasionally publish humorous pieces, but they sometimes take themselves a bit too seriously. Literary publishers are concerned with a piece's style, imagery, and characterization. Plot is not so overwhelmingly important here.

With few exceptions, commercial and literary publishers have very little to do with one another, and usually a piece that will interest one group of publishers won't interest the other. Neither group has much respect for the other, or for what the other publishes, and editors in one area are typically unimpressed (and sometimes unfavorably impressed) by writers who have published work in the other.

At the very top of the publishing heap these distinctions disappear. Magazines like *Harper's, The New Yorker, The Atlantic,* and a very few others stand with one leg in commercial publishing and another in literary publishing. Some of the best book publishers, such as Farrar, Straus & Giroux, North Point Press, Alfred A. Knopf, and a handful of others do the same. Publishing commercial works enables them to afford to publish the more literary material.

If you're interested in being published, which area of publishing should you write for? Neither. Write whatever you want to write; when it's done, send it to those publications (literary, commercial, or both) that will provide the most appropriate showcase or have the audience you most want to reach.

Writer's Block

MUCH HAS BEEN written about the supposed horrors of what is called "writer's block." As a result, many writers—particularly new writers—have a morbid fear of being struck down in their prime by this dreaded condition.

In truth, "writer's block" is a rather generic label that is put on a variety of conditions, any one of which can have dozens of different causes. Writer's block can refer to the inability to finish a particular piece; the inability to finish *any* piece of writing; the general inability to write well; or the inability to confront the blank page at all.

The most important thing to understand about writer's block is that it is almost never serious or long-lasting. It can usually be cured without too much effort; and even when no cure works, it usually goes away by itself after a few days or, at most, a week or two. If you've been worrying about writer's block, stop worrying—even if you've got it right now.

The most common cause of any of the blocks described above is *something other than writing*: overwork, physical or emotional stress, illness or convalescence, poor diet, poor or too little sleep, excessive worry or distraction, changes or disruption in your routine, inadequate conditions for writing (such as poor lighting or ventilation, too little room, or too much noise), drinking or drug use, or a personal problem (e.g., a death in the family or a recent fight with your spouse).

In such cases, the way to cure your block is to resolve the particular problem that is causing it. For example, if you're upset about your daughter's illness, your inability to write may be a side effect of your concern for her. You need to either stop worrying about her or accept the block until she is healthy again. Or suppose you have trouble writing during hay fever season; perhaps the medication you're taking for your allergy is dulling your creative abilities. Try altering the dosage; or write only as the drug begins to wear off.

Writer's block can in some cases be natural and normal. You'll recall from chapters 20 and 65 that some writers have natural rhythms that include "on" periods and "off" periods; during "off" periods these writers can (and should) do little or no writing. Writer's block may well be a natural part of your own creative cycle. (Speaking of cycles, some women may experience writer's block at certain points in their menstrual cycles.)

Writer's block can, of course, be partly or entirely caused by the particular piece you are working on. You might have written yourself into a corner; or you might be thinking repeatedly along the same unproductive line; or you might simply be weary of working on that project and need a break. If you are stuck somewhere in a story or poem, reread chapter 63, Getting Unstuck, and try some of its suggestions for unsticking yourself. Chapters 56, 59, 62, 64, and 65 can also supply useful suggestions.

OTHER CAUSES OF writer's block and their solutions:

• Cause: asking or expecting too much of yourself, either in your writing or in your life in general. Solution: go easier on yourself. Relax.

• Cause: a strong conscious or subconscious desire to be doing something else. Solutions: 1) Make writing, or the writing of that particular piece, as comfortable and pleasant as possible. Break it up into one-hour sessions, or write in bed, or keep a bottle of wine beside you. 2) Plan to reward yourself with something you like a great deal once the project is finished. Follow through on this promise to yourself once the piece is done. If you need to use the reward system at one or more intermediate stages as well, that's fine. 3) Do something else. If you really detest working on a particular piece, perhaps you're better off not working on it at all.

• Cause: a distaste for writing in general. Solutions: 1) Stop writing. Do something else. Why make yourself miserable? Your time will be better spent doing something you enjoy. 2) Force yourself. (Not generally recommended.)

• Cause: laziness. Solution: Admit that you're being lazy; then get off your duff and start writing. Any mental arguments or conversations on this topic are themselves forms of laziness and avoidance; scuttle (or at least ignore) them and write.

• Cause: fear of writing. Solution: Reread chapter 2 of this book.

IF WRITER'S BLOCK, in any of its forms, occurs to you frequently, you might want to examine your life in general, to see if the block is connected to anything specific in it (e.g., a certain food, a particular person's presence, a certain time of day, or the weather).

Some writers like to end each writing session in the middle of a sentence, line, or stanza. Their thoughts are thus already started when they next return to writing. This helps them avoid writer's block in the first place.

92

Writing for Children

WRITING FOR CHILDREN is exactly like writing for adults. The same rules and standards apply; you have the same options, possibilities, and freedoms; you may use an equally wide variety of forms, styles, and approaches; and the same processes and procedures apply. The only limitations are in vocabulary and themes.

The biggest mistake you can make when writing for children is writing down to them. *Never* insult or underestimate your reader's intelligence, especially if your reader is under the age of sixteen. Kids hate being condescended to, even if their parents don't mind.

Being cutesy is another big mistake. By cutesy, I mean something like this: "Gosh, thought Mr. Tree, that Mr. Squirrel certainly is fluffy! I wish my branches had fur on them, so they'd be soft and cuddly just like Mr. Squirrel is. Oh, look! There goes Mr. Squirrel now, hopping through the forest." This sort of writing bores kids, and it may also make them gag. (Actually, a tree wanting to have fur on its branches instead of leaves is not a half bad idea. But for the story to work, it would need to be written as simply, clearly, and concisely as possible—just like a story for adults.)

OTHER TIPS ON writing for children:
- The vocabulary in your piece should be appropriate for

your audience, just as it should be in a piece written for adults. In practice, it is not usually a good idea to try to write on a particular vocabulary level. Instead, write the piece just as you normally would; then, *as you rewrite and polish it,* go through it to catch words and sentences that are too advanced for your readers. Replace those words or rewrite those sentences.

• Kids have shorter attention spans than most adults. If your piece is a long one, you may want to break it up into short chapters or sections. In general, the lower the age of your audience, the shorter those chapters or sections should be.

• Kids are much more willing to take something fantastic on faith, without explanation or qualification. For instance, you could get away with starting a children's story like this: "Megan, a fourteen-year-old dragon, was president of IBM." But you'd have a very hard time starting a story—even a science fiction story—for adults that way.

• Children are human beings. They have the same feelings as adults—with, of course, the exception of erotic feelings in younger kids. Treat them as young human beings, not as members of a separate, ignorant and/or innocent species.

• Certain themes are clearly inappropriate for kids. *Explicit* sex and violence should be avoided, at least in pieces for kids under twelve or thirteen, though there's nothing wrong with mentioning that your characters fought battles or made love.

• This does not mean you can't deal with touchy or difficult subjects. It is permissible to discuss things such as divorce, alcoholism, and even physical or sexual abuse, *provided you use a vocabulary and approach that your young readers can benefit from.* Anything prurient or lurid, however, is of course out of the question.

93

Finding a Second Critic

YOU READ IN chapter 57 how to locate one or more critics for your work and how to make best use of their comments. If you haven't started showing some of your writing to at least one person already, now is a good time to do so.

If you *have* already been getting criticism from someone, now is likely a good time to begin looking for a second critic. But don't get rid of the first one; now that you have some experience as a writer under your belt, it's useful to begin getting two or more different opinions on at least some of your work.

Why two or more opinions? Isn't one informed judgment enough?

At this stage in your development as a writer it unfortunately isn't, even if that judgment is as close to ideal as possible. For one thing, it's easy to become dependent on the ideas and criticisms of a single critic if that's the only person you bring your work to. In fact, it's possible to subconsciously begin writing the kind of pieces you think that critic will enjoy. Furthermore, the judgments of your first critic, no matter how useful they may be, are nevertheless informed in part by his or her tastes. Having a second critic will enable you to differentiate between legitimate criticisms and those that reflect taste more than judgment.

A second critic may also be able to offer insights and suggestions that the first cannot, since he will bring his own unique experience, background, and perspective to your work.

Having at least two critics look at your work will also broaden *your own* perspective. You'll get a firsthand look at how intelligent people can disagree, sometimes completely; how intelligent people can sometimes be wrong; and how differently two people can view the same piece of writing. Having two opinions to consider (and sometimes combine, and sometimes weigh against one another) will also help you make your own decisions about rewriting and polishing your work.

As you know by now, the final decision of how any of your pieces is written or rewritten is your own. The whole point of asking for criticism from others is not to replace your own best judgment but to give you useful input for making your own final decisions.

You can find a second critic the same way you found the first. You should use the same criteria in selecting that critic and in listening to and considering his or her comments.

Let each critic know that you will also be showing your work to the other; also let the first critic know that you are not seeking another opinion because his or her comments haven't been useful. Instead, explain the importance of getting a second perspective—or, if you like, show the person this chapter.

Important: *never* play one critic against the other. It's fine to show the same piece to both people, but *never* tell one critic, "Well, Melissa liked the piece even if you don't" or "Fred thought the last stanza was the *best* part." Listen to each critic's comments carefully, without argument. If necessary, ask for details and clarification. *Don't* set up debates between your critics, either directly or through you; this benefits no one.

As always, if you want to stop seeking a particular critic's reactions to your work, for whatever reason, that is absolutely your right.

EXERCISE #24

GET COMFORTABLE AND prepare yourself to write. Have plenty of paper and (if you use pen or pencil to write) one or two extra writing implements available.

Get a clock, watch, or timer and place it nearby. Give yourself exactly forty minutes to write, beginning at a particular moment.

Start writing. Once you've started, don't stop. Keep the words coming and physically keep your fingers moving.

If you get stuck, repeat the previous line, phrase, or sentence until something else comes to mind. Don't worry if what you write doesn't look so great or if a good deal of it is gibberish or repetition.

If, when you begin, you have nothing in mind to write about, begin with any sentence or line chosen at random and keep repeating it until something comes to you.

Continue writing for the full forty minutes. When the time is up, you may continue writing if you wish, until you come to a natural stopping point, or until you begin to naturally wind down.

Once you have finished, look over what you have written. Get rid of any gibberish (there will likely be quite a lot). Look through the rest of what you have done, noting the good ideas, lines, or images.

If, by the end of the forty minutes, you have gotten a piece going, wonderful. Continue writing it, either now or at some future time.

If, after forty minutes, you haven't gotten going on a piece, look through what you've written and use something from that material as the basis for beginning a story, poem, or other piece of creative writing.

THINGS TO KEEP in mind:

● Because you have to keep writing, you may feel that you have to write very fast. This isn't necessary, nor is it usually helpful. Instead, write as slowly and steadily as you like—though if writing fast does come naturally to you, go ahead and write fast.

● You may vary the time limit as you see fit. If forty minutes seems too long, give yourself thirty. But vary the time limit *before* you start writing. Once you actually begin writing, don't stop until the prearranged amount of time is up.

● It's easy to become nervous while doing this exercise because you have to keep writing. But it is very possible to do this exercise in a relaxed way. Make sure you're physically comfortable as you write. Take it slow and easy. Don't try to force images and ideas to come. Let them come naturally, and let yourself repeat the same line or sentence forty times if you have to.

94

A Do-It-Yourself Writers' Workshop

ONE EXCELLENT WAY to get feedback on your work, and to simultaneously meet other writers, is to form a writers' workshop or join an existing one.

Writers' workshops typically meet at regular intervals, usually once a week to once a month. Meetings last one to three hours, during which the group discusses manuscripts submitted by members.

A writer wanting criticism on a particular piece photocopies or dittos one copy of that piece for each workshop member; copies are distributed at the next workshop meeting; and the piece is discussed at the meeting after that.

A workshop is as useful or useless, as lively or dull, and as intelligent or slow-witted as its members. As you might expect, the criticism can range from brilliant to silly—not only from workshop to workshop, but from member to member, and occasionally even from meeting to meeting. As time passes, you'll get to know which members of the group tend to provide the most useful criticism and which ones tend to spout nonsense.

It isn't too difficult to start a writers' workshop on your own. Simply put up small signs on local bulletin boards or put an ad in your local paper. If there's a writers' center in your area, post a notice there, or run an ad in its newsletter. (The center may itself run one or more workshops, or keep a list of people looking to form them.) The first meeting can be at your home; later meetings can be at whatever location the group chooses.

Workshops can be as small as three people or as large as fifteen. (Workshops of more than fifteen people become time-consuming and unwieldy, and they don't easily fit into people's living rooms and rec rooms.) Each workshop session should have a leader; a single leader can be chosen for a set period of time, or the leaderships can rotate from month to month, session to session, or piece to piece. No one should act as workshop leader, however, while one of his or her manuscripts is being discussed and criticized.

Here is the procedure I have used with great success in writing workshops in the past:

All the participants are seated in such a way that they can all see one another. A circle is usually best.

The leader's job is to loosely direct the discussion and make sure it doesn't stray off its topic. (If it does, the leader should interrupt and bring it back.) The leader also watches the clock to make sure the meeting ends more or less on time; he or she reminds the group of the time remaining, and when necessary speeds up the discussion. The leader has no other powers or responsibility, nor should he or she assume any.

Only one manuscript is discussed at a time. The leader begins the discussion by asking the author to read a section of the piece aloud; if the piece is short enough, he or she may read the entire piece. (Note: this step is optional. I tend to use it with poetry but not with prose.)

The leader then calls for comments. People may respond as they like, without first requesting permission to speak; but when someone gets interrupted, talked over, or shouted down, the leader should cut in and say, "Let the speaker finish." If someone wants to speak but other people keep speaking first, the leader should say, "Wait a minute, let's hear from ____."

The comments of the first person who speaks will deter-

270

mine the first general topic of the discussion. *However, it must be understood by all workshop members that the discussion will begin with the most important topics and end with the least important ones.* Important topics include plot, style, approach, characterization, central imagery, central symbols and/or metaphors, meaning or message, form, and so on.

HERE ARE SOME examples of good opening comments:
- "It's not clear to me why Joe is so affected by the call from his sister in the climax."
- "Theresa and Ralph seem like real people, but Melinda seems two-dimensional."
- "I don't think that the central image of water and ice works in this poem."
- "This piece is written in the first person past, but I wonder if it would be stronger if it were written in the third person present."
- "This poem wants to be funny, but the only funny part is the first stanza."

These are the kinds of comments that provoke serious and productive discussion. They deal with central issues and raise important questions. Most of the discussion of any piece should be on issues such as these.

Any criticism (or item of praise) should be backed up by one or more specific references to the piece under discussion. For example, "Look at the dialogue on page six. Theresa and Ralph speak like real New Yorkers, but Melinda talks like she's reading a newspaper aloud."

Comments like "I really think you should have said 'man' instead of 'gentleman'" or "I don't get the joke about dogs" should be saved for the end of the discussion. This not only puts each aspect of the discussion in order of decreasing priority, it assures that if time runs out before the discussion is complete, the central issues have been addressed. (If minor comments get brought up too soon, the leader should ask the speaker to hold them until later.) Issues such as the effectiveness of individual scenes, stanzas, or descriptions are of moderate importance, and should be brought up toward the middle of the discussion.

If no one volunteers, the leader may begin with a comment of his or her own.

Once discussion has begun on a particular topic, it should continue on that topic until everyone who has something to say about it has had a chance to talk. Comments on other topics should be held until the appropriate time; when necessary, the leader should remind speakers of this.

After a topic has been thoroughly discussed, the leader should ask for comments on another topic. This next topic might already have been determined by the previous discussion; if not, the leader may either suggest the next topic, ask for suggestions for the next topic, or simply call for further discussion and let the subject be determined by whoever speaks next.

This process continues, topic by topic, from the most important points and issues to the least, until everyone has said what he or she wants to say—or until the discussion is no longer productive and the leader calls it to a halt.

People may speak as much or as little, and as often or as infrequently, as they please. However, no one should monopolize the discussion or continue for too long; if necessary, the leader should ask a talkative speaker to let others say their pieces.

Criticism involves both positive and negative comments—and neutral ones, too. Group members should not only point out what isn't working and why it isn't; they should praise those things about a piece that succeed and explain how and why they succeed. Anyone who is uniformly negative, or who seems to enjoy tearing apart others' work, should be told to leave the group.

Disagreement among members should be permitted. But once the appropriate points have been made, they should not be belabored; the leader should get the discussion moving forward once again.

Lively discussion and debate should be encouraged; arguments and fights must not be. The leader should stop any shouting matches, name-calling, and personal attacks *immediately*.

Here is perhaps the most important point of all: no one must *ever* criticize the *author* of a piece. The discussion must be limited entirely to the manuscript at hand. Comments like "only a bleeding heart liberal could have written this" or "did the author have a bad experience as a policeman, or what?" are way out of line. They are irrelevant; they may be insulting; and they are probably none of anybody's business.

Once a point has been made, it need not—and should not—be reiterated in detail by others. Group members who agree should simply say something like, "I feel the same way as Jim about the dialogue."

The leader should save all of his own comments until the discussion of a piece is complete, at which point he should give them all in one fell swoop. This is simply to avoid confusion and conflicting roles during the discussion. He should avoid repeating any points that have already been made, and his presentation should normally take no more than five or ten minutes.

Throughout the entire discussion, and throughout the leader's concluding remarks, *the author must remain silent*. This is extremely important, as it keeps the discussion on track and avoids having the whole thing devolve into a question-and-answer session or a debate. In certain cases, it may also keep the author from blowing his or her top.

If, during the discussion, someone wants to ask the author a question, he or she may do so; if the question has a simple answer (e.g., "Did you mean 'boy' or 'bog' here?"), the author may answer it. If the question does not have a simple answer, however (e.g., "Why are there two robbers instead of one?"), the author may not respond until all discussion is complete.

Once everyone (including the leader) has spoken, the author should be given a few minutes to respond—if he or she chooses. (If he or she has nothing to say, or just wants to say "Thanks for the insights," this is fine.) During this time everyone else must remain silent.

The author should *not* use this time (normally about ten minutes, fifteen at the outside) to defend his piece or himself —though he may, if he wishes, explain his intentions, clarify why he chose a particular approach, image, or technique, or answer questions put to him earlier. He may *not* in any way attack his fellow workshop members or their comments. For example, he may not say, "Howard's comments on the icicle scene are ridiculous" or "I think Amy's dead wrong about the dance stanza." In listening to everyone's comments, the author should follow the advice in chapter 34.

Finally, the other group members may ask the author questions about the piece; any questions asked earlier that have gone unanswered may be asked again. The author may respond to each question as he or she pleases, including by declining to respond. ("I'd prefer not to answer that" will do nicely, and should be respected by workshop members. No one should ever be forced or required to respond to any question.)

The group members then pass their copies of the manuscript, on which they have previously written comments at home, to the author. (He or she can study these later, after the workshop session is over.) The group then moves on to the next manuscript.

This procedure has worked very well for my students over the years; however, feel free to modify it as you like, or to develop a separate procedure of your own, to suit your particular group.

Though writers' workshops can be helpful, they are not for everyone. If you feel uncomfortable having your work discussed by a group, or if you prefer working one-on-one with a critic, there's no reason in the world why you have to subject yourself to a workshop. But for other writers, a workshop can be encouraging, inspiring, and energizing. It can also be a good way to meet new friends with similar interests.

Ideally, a writers' workshop functions in part as a classroom, offering writers a small but interested audience and valuable criticism of their work. But it also functions as a support group, where writers can meet and talk with other writers, and where the act of writing is understood, accepted, and respected.

95

Submitting Your Work to Editors

IF YOU'VE WRITTEN something that you feel is good enough to be published, you may wish to send it to editors for possible publication.

Getting published, or trying to get published, does not make you more of a writer, nor does it make you a better one. You needn't feel any obligation to try to publish your work, now or ever. As you learned in chapter 89, a published piece is not necessarily better than an unpublished one. However, if you'd like to send your work to editors, the following guidelines should be extremely useful.

First, keep in mind that the great majority of manuscripts, especially those by new writers, get rejected—no matter how good they may be. Most often you will get a form rejection letter; if you get a personal letter, this means the editor felt your piece had some real merit.

Second, editors will rarely explain why they are rejecting a piece, nor should you expect them to. If they do supply a reason, don't assume they're right (or wrong); evaluate their comments using the suggestions in chapter 34.

For poetry and short prose pieces, it is wise to start out small—with neighborhood and local newspapers, local and regional magazines, small literary journals, and/or genre magazines such as *Hitchcock's Mystery Magazine, Asimov's Science Fiction Magazine,* and so on. It is *much* easier for a new writer to be published in these periodicals than in magazines with large readerships and/or international reputations. Once you've published a few pieces in these smaller publications, you can try your work at larger and better-known ones (e.g., *Yankee, Field, Omni, The Antioch Review,* the smaller-circulation women's magazines). Then, once you've published a few pieces in these mid-range periodicals, you can shoot for publication in *The New Yorker, Antaeus, Harper's, The Paris Review, Redbook, Penthouse,* and so on.

You are welcome to ignore this advice and start at the top (or the middle) if you wish, but the chances of getting your work accepted are extremely slim.

When submitting work for publication, always send it to the appropriate editor *by name,* not by title—e.g., to Sally Monk, not to Fiction Editor. You can find the proper editor's name in any periodical (except *The New Yorker* and a few very large newspapers) by checking its list of staff members. This is usually published near the front of each issue. (For the addresses of book publishers and the names of their editors, see the current edition of the annual reference book *Literary Market Place,* available in most libraries.)

Each submission should include your manuscript(s), a brief cover letter, a self-addressed envelope large enough for the return of the manuscript(s), and first-class return postage (or the equivalent in International Reply Coupons, if the manuscript is being sent out of the country. Reply coupons are available at most post offices). Use typed address labels on both your submission envelope and your return envelope.

Your manuscript should be neatly typed, on one side of the page only, on white 8½" x 11" paper. Use a clean black ribbon that makes neat, dark letters; do *not* use script or other strange typefaces. Don't use onion skin, erasable paper, or any paper with holes or lines. Photocopy or ditto (spirit duplicating) paper are both excellent; these are available cheaply by the ream (five hundred sheets) from office supply stores.

Manuscripts should be neat in appearance and very easy to read. Each line of each piece should be carefully proofread. Small errors may be corrected in pen or pencil. If a page has large errors, or several small ones, it should probably be retyped.

Proper use of a photocopying machine can save you retyping time, however. If you carefully cut pages apart and tape them together, then photocopy this page, the result will look as good as a freshly typed page. You can also use correction tape to cover errors. This is sticky white tape of various widths from about 1/3″ up, available at office supply stores. Simply place a strip of tape over a line you wish to correct, then type the proper line on the tape. The tape won't show up on the photocopy—only the clear, crisp typed text.

Manuscripts typed on computer printers must be letter-quality; many editors are unwilling to read dot-matrix and "near letter-quality" manuscripts, and even those that are willing aren't happy about doing it.

Make photocopies of each manuscript. Keep the original for yourself; send the photocopies to editors. This way you are safe in the event an editor loses your manuscript—something which happens much too often.

Prose manuscripts should be double-spaced; poetry should be single-spaced or one and a half-spaced, with an additional space between stanzas. Each poem should be typed (or begun) on a separate page. A sample of the precise manuscript form for prose appears on pages 279-80; the manuscript form for poetry appears on pages 281-82. Note in each case the proper placement of your name, address, telephone number(s), and title. In a prose manuscript *only,* the number of words and your telephone number should be indicated. The number of words should be rounded off to the nearest 100 (to the nearest 500 for manuscripts of 3000 words or more).

Margins should be about one inch on all four sides.

SAMPLE FIRST PAGE OF PROSE MANUSCRIPT

Scott Edelstein
2706 West 43 Street, Suite 102
Minneapolis, MN 55410
(612) 929-9123

About 4500 words

COMFORT

by Scott Edelstein

Ever since I was a little boy, my mother suffered from chronic headaches. She'd usually get them in late afternoon, especially when the days were hot and muggy. She hated to take pills, and when one of her headaches would set in, she'd lie down on her bed, close her eyes, and have my father sit beside her and rub her forehead. Almost always, the headaches would go away after a few minutes of rubbing. This impressed me immensely, and probably had something to do with my becoming a massage therapist fifteen years later. From the start, however, my mother had wanted me to be a doctor.

One hot, thick summer afternoon when I was six, my mother called me up to her bedroom. My father was away in Columbus on business, and she said to me, "Bobby, would you like to try rubbing my head for me?"

"Sure," I said, delighted at the chance to do a grownup's job.

"Sit next to me," she said, "and put your fingers on my temples." Her eyes

Edelstein/2

were closed and she looked very pale. I put my dirty hands on her forehead, but I didn't know where the temples were. She reached up and repositioned my hands, then showed me how to rub. "See?" she said. "In circles. Press down, but not too hard. It's a bad one, so rub carefully." Then she put her hand back down at her side.

I started rubbing as best I could. She kept her eyes closed and her mouth was open just a little.

I worked on her forehead until I was tired and bored. Then I said, "Is it any better, Mom?"

She smiled slightly and lifted my hands off her forehead. "A little." She sat up, then squeezed her eyes shut tightly and lay back down again. "Are you okay?" I asked. She didn't answer.

I started rubbing again, but after a few seconds she sat back up, much more slowly, and propped herself up on her arms. "I'm going to get some water," she said in a whisper. She stood up very carefully, wobbled for a second, and then walked slowly out of the bedroom, holding her right arm half outstretched in front of her.

I lay down on the bed and wiggled my legs impatiently, singing a TV commercial to myself. Then I heard my mother groan, and there was a horrible plop as she collapsed in the hallway.

I ran out into the hall and saw her lying unconscious, her body limp and twisted up.

I'd never seen anyone in a faint before, and I didn't know what to do. I panicked. I began running back and forth between my mother and the bedroom, screaming.

Mrs. Baum next door heard me through the open window, and she hurried

SAMPLE FIRST PAGE OF POETRY MANUSCRIPT

John Edward Sorrel
111 Avenue Street
City, NY   10000

SHELTER

The sun falls all afternoon, to earth;
Lands behind these spring elms; but can't hold
Earth's precarious edge where they root,
Draws the elms with it, down into dark.

    In the bright dark Beth and I'd hold hands tight,
Sweaty--suck, suck, and crack great big red-hots
Called Atomic Fireballs--as, onscreen, Sarge
Flashed and swept whole nests of Japs, no sweat.

    Cross-stepping back home to her house, we'd stop
Short--testing each other--quick, skip the crack:
To fix her dad's back. He'd be standing watch
Against the window with his bottle.

    Forever the red-checked tablecloth, stained.
He'd say just wipe spills off, never make us
Eat our greens, never make us anything
Much, but hamburgers, hot dogs, and beans.

    In class, at the bomb drill's clang, we'd all jump
Under our desks--but Beth. She'd jump in
With me, us giggling--till, late May, Miss Raines
Yanked us out, called down Beth's dad. Who just stared.

    At last muttered what difference did it make
If we held hands at the final flash--
That week, backed their station wagon up,
Stacked two by fours, lugged big rough gray blocks.

    Murmured over his scraped knuckles, bad back,
Told Miss Raines to go scream bloody murder
At Beth's mother, not him, they could both scream
Their heads off at a little girl who's scared.

SAMPLE SECOND PAGE OF POETRY MANUSCRIPT

He kicked the spade. We climbed from the elms. Hands
Scooped dirt, scooped, till eyes met earth's edge. He said
Here we were, planting ourselves, roof of stars
Sprouting up from us, deep, our shelter.

We dug our own hole back by the woods,
Built our shelter walls deep with his scraps.
We'd pull his old study door, our roof, tight.
One day, peeled her blouse, my shirt, and tested.

    Late, tiptoed in: By the night light's faint glow,
    He still stood watch, rubbing his back, bottle
    In one arm, half cradled, bare undershirt
    Soaked black with sweat. In the window mirrored
    Pale and dark, he softly rocked; hoarse, murmured
    How stars now sheltered towns, they'd never drop
    The bomb, never bomb our street thick with elms—
    Where they dropped it, the earth waved with tall palms—
    So far down, that if they just had let him
    Fly by the stars, he'd have flown on, on by
    The huddled, pinned lights of towns and dropped
    Nothing, not the first light flashing out
    So far down, no screams from those tiny fires
    So far down, no one could have caught him—
    His own wife didn't know him anymore.

Beth's palm soothes my knuckles. We stand watch.
Our elms will rise again with dawn, sun
Flash the earth's edge, climb to lose that edge
And shelter us with calm morning light.

She winces; then smiles. She lays and presses
My hand on her warm, round swell: I feel our child
        Deep within, kick,
          Testing.

      —

At the top of each page except the first, indicate the page number and either your last name or the title of the piece.

Only one prose manuscript should normally be submitted to an editor at a time; however, you may send two very short (under one thousand words) prose manuscripts to the same editor in the same envelope. *Short* poems and prose poems should not be sent singly, but three to six at a time; if some poems are longer than one page, the total batch should be no more than ten to twelve pages. Poems longer than this length should be sent individually.

Manuscripts should be held together by a paper clip of appropriate size, *not* by staples or any kind of binding. Your cover letter should be placed inside the clip, on top of the manuscript(s); the return envelope should also be placed inside the clip, at the rear of the manuscript. Return first-class postage may be either affixed to the return envelope or placed under the paper clip on top of the cover letter.

Manuscripts should normally be sent flat, in a 9″ x 12″ (or larger) envelope. Submissions should be sent first class mail; those going outside of North America should normally be sent airmail.

Your cover letter should be brief, businesslike, and to the point. A sample letter appears on page 284. Your second paragraph should list any appropriate previous (or forth-coming) publications, and any other *appropriate* background information (e.g., a literary award, a decade spent researching the subject of your piece, an M.F.A. degree in writing). If you have no such credits or credentials to list, eliminate this paragraph entirely.

If you are sending a batch of poems, it is neither necessary nor appropriate to list them by title in your cover letter.

You may send the same story or poem to more than one publication at a time; however, as soon as you agree to let one editor publish it, you must *immediately* write or call the other editors who have the piece and withdraw it from their consideration. (If a publication is willing to reprint material that

SAMPLE COVER LETTER

92 Annapolis Lane
Minneapolis, MN 55404
(612) 990-4140

March 2, 1987

Ms. Eileen Clement
The Hypothetical Review
2248 Wendell Road
Portland, ME 01775

Dear Eileen Clement:

I've been writing short fiction for the past three years, and reading and enjoying The Hypothetical Review for the past five. I thought one of my most recent stories, "Partridges," might be right for your magazine, so I'm enclosing it now. I'm also enclosing a return envelope and return postage.

My earlier work has appeared, or is scheduled to appear, in The Example, The Imaginary Quarterly, and Assumption. I have an M.F.A. in Creative Writing from the University of Columbus, and I'm currently at work on a novel.

I look forward to your reply.

Sincerely,

Martin Jacobs

has appeared elsewhere, then you need not withdraw it from that publication.)

Replies normally take about one to three months. After three months without a reply, you may write or call an editor to ask about a manuscript's status.

THESE ARE THE basics of submitting your work for publication. There is, however, a great deal more that can be said on the subject, as well as on the subjects of dealing with editors, researching markets, and understanding and negotiating publishing contracts. For complete details on these topics and many others related to writing for publication, see my book *The Indispensable Writer's Guide* (Harper & Row).

Publishing your work isn't the only way you can present it to an audience. Public readings are another excellent option; many libraries, bookstores, colleges and universities, community centers, writers' centers, and other community-service organizations sponsor readings by poets and fiction writers. Some have reading series that bring local and national writers in on a regular basis to read their work aloud. Another possibility is an informal reading, perhaps in your own home, for family and friends. It isn't the size of the audience that counts, but how interested it is in your work.

96

Writing as a Career

MANY PEOPLE ENJOY writing so much that they consider making it into a career. If you are contemplating such a career, keep the following things in mind:

- There are two kinds of writing careers: in a salaried position (as a journalist, speechwriter, advertising writer, public relations writer, technical writer, etc.); and freelancing, in which you write for a variety of different publications and are your own boss. Salaried writing jobs (and writing-related jobs such as editing, proofreading, etc.) are not terribly difficult for good writers to land. These jobs do sometimes require specific training, however. Freelance writing, while much more glamorous, usually yields much less money and much less financial security. *Very* few freelancers are able to support themselves entirely by their writing. The vast majority of freelancers also hold part-time or full-time jobs.

- It is extraordinarily difficult—not impossible, but rather close to it—to break into writing for television and film. The money in both is excellent, but the competition is enormous, and the odds are heavily against you.

- It is not usually easy for a new writer to get published. The more you do publish, however, the less difficult further publication becomes.

- There is virtually no money to be earned publishing

poetry. There are at most six poets in the United States who actually make their livings from publishing verse.

• An excellent book on this subject is *Career Opportunities for Writers* by Rosemary Guiley (Facts on File). This volume describes a wide variety of salaried writing jobs, including the opportunities, salary, and necessary qualifications for each. For details on *freelance* writing as a career, and freelance jobs in related fields, see my book *The Indispensable Writer's Guide* (Harper & Row).

97

Vanity Publishing and Other Schemes

NO DOUBT YOU'VE seen ads in writers' magazines, other magazines and newspapers, and perhaps even your Yellow Pages, that begin "Writers Wanted," "To the Author in Search of a Publisher," or "Become a Published Author." These ads encourage writers to submit their work to certain publishers for free evaluations.

These ads are normally placed by firms known as *vanity publishers*: publishers who will publish virtually any level of writing for a fee. There are dozens of these publishers in North America.

If you send your work to one of these publishers, you will most likely get back an enthusiastic reply; the publisher will offer to publish your manuscript—*if* you will put up a large sum of money (typically around $10,000 for a 300-page book) to pay for the book's publication, promotion, and distribution.

Vanity publishing is not illegal, and it is not an attempt to swindle: your work will be duly published, promoted (at least to some extent), and made available to bookstores just as your contract stipulates. However, chances are slim that your work will sell more than a few copies.

Think about it. Vanity publishers will publish almost anything that comes their way, no matter how awful, provided that its author is willing to pay hard cash for its publication. The result is that very few bookstores will order many books from vanity publishers, because they know full well that their books are often quite awful. This catch-22 almost guarantees that your book will sell poorly.

Then there is what is called *subsidy publishing*. This is where a company that normally publishes books at its own expense offers to publish, promote, and distribute a book, provided its author (or someone else) will put up some or all of the money to do so. This arrangement isn't offered often, particularly by major publishing firms, but it does happen. One writer I know sent his manuscript to a mid-sized publisher that had recently published several well-known writers; he received an enthusiastic reply from an editor who wanted to publish his book, but the firm first wanted $20,000 to cover the costs of its publication.

Subsidy publishing is a far better arrangement than vanity publishing, since in most cases the publishing firm has a decent reputation among bookstores and a competent staff of sales and promotion people. However, even subsidy publishing is normally inferior to mainstream publishing, where publication costs you nothing and you might earn some money.

A variation on vanity and subsidy publishing is mail-order poetry anthologies. Perhaps you've seen the ads in writers' magazines that begin "Poets Wanted" or "Attention Poets." These ads solicit poems for anthologization; some of the ads also mention poetry contests with cash prizes. These ads normally come from firms that publish annual or semiannual mail-order anthologies. These anthologies are usually hardcover, handsomely made, and very large—five hundred 8½" x 11" pages is typical. Each anthology contains over a thousand, perhaps even several thousand, poems. Virtually any poem, no matter how awful, will be included in such an anthology so long as it is not pornographic and does not advocate illegal acts. The author is informed that his or

289

her poem has been accepted for publication and is offered copies of the anthology at a special price—say, $35 per copy. Here's the catch: usually the author *must* purchase at least one copy of the anthology, or the poem may not be published. (No free authors' copies are distributed, of course.) To keep the publisher's profits high, each author is limited to one poem per anthology.

These anthologies are normally available only by mail-order, directly from the publisher. Few or no bookstores carry them. I generally urge my students to avoid mail-order poetry anthologies.

If you don't know whether or not a particular company is a vanity publisher, check the reference book *Literary Market Place,* which is available in most libraries. Vanity presses are never listed in *LMP,* though some presses that do subsidy publishing are.

The editors of most reputable anthologies, magazines, and book publishers do not advertise for stories and poems; rather, they run notices in the "markets" columns of writers' magazines.

Another common variation on the theme of vanity publishing is contests that require entry fees. There are now dozens of such literary contests throughout North America, and they cover every possible genre of writing. Typically, the winner of such a contest receives a cash prize (anywhere from $100 to $1000) and publication of his or her manuscript. There may also be a second and, perhaps, a third prize. However, to enter a manuscript, the writer must pay an entry fee, usually between $5 and $10. These fees are used to pay the winners their prizes and to pay for publication of the winning manuscript. Often these contests also make a profit for their sponsors.

These contests differ from vanity publishing arrangements in one important respect: in *some* (though by no means all) cases they are sponsored by reputable publishers, often connected with colleges or universities, whose books and magazines find their way onto bookstore and library shelves. Before entering one of these contests, you would do well to determine whether or not the sponsor has a reputation as a serious and reasonably well-known publisher.

There is another variation on this theme that has become more and more common in the past few years: the reading fee. This is a fee charged to authors by publishers simply to have their manuscripts *considered* for publication. Fees range from a dollar or two for shorter works to ten dollars or more for book-length manuscripts. Here again, the fees are used to help keep the publishing operations going. Most such fees are charged by small literary publishers, some of which are highly reputable, some of which are not.

In general, there's little reason why you should pay to have your work published or considered. The vast majority of publishers do not charge money to authors for either manuscript consideration or publication. Many writers choose to deal only with these publishers.

If you are willing to pay to get your work into print, however, and/or if you have had no success in getting your work published by mainstream publishers, you may want to look into self-publishing. This is the practice of arranging and paying for the publication and distribution of your work yourself. If you self-publish your work, you must handle all the details yourself, including promoting and selling your work to readers, bookstores, libraries, etc. You must also pay for all the costs of typesetting, layout, printing, binding, advertising, and distribution. However, you retain complete control over how your work is designed, printed, sold, and distributed, and all the money you receive from sales of your work belongs to you.

For details on self-publishing, see one or more of these books:

The Complete Guide to Self-Publishing by Tom and Marilyn Ross (Writer's Digest Books).

The Self-Publishing Manual by Dan Poynter (Para Publishing).

The Publish-It-Yourself Handbook by Bill Henderson (Pushcart Press).

How to Publish, Promote, and Sell Your Own Book by Robert L. Holt (St. Martin's Press).

Most self-publishing is done on a small scale, though a few writers have become famous or rich by publishing their own work. Anaïs Nin began by publishing her own writings. Other well-known writers who have been self-published include Herman Melville, Avram Davidson, and Peter McWilliams.

EXERCISE #25

TAKE A FEW minutes to consider what it is you most like to read. This might involve specific genres (mystery, science fiction, mythology, humor, etc.); specific themes or ideas (pieces about politics, pieces about animals, pieces with tragic endings, and so on); specific forms (experimental pieces, sonnets, memoirs, etc.), or some combination of the three.

Now take a few minutes to imagine the single piece of writing that would most thrill or excite you; the thing you would most like to read; the story, poem, or other piece of writing that would give you the most pleasure or satisfaction.

Now, write that piece.

THINGS TO KEEP in mind:

• If the task of writing your own ideal story or poem scares you or seems too difficult, try writing it anyway. You may find, to your surprise, that you have the talent and skills to pull it off. And if, after giving it a sincere and wholehearted try, you realize you can't pull it off, what have you lost? Remember, too, to save what you have written. You can always come back to it in the future. You may well find that, a few months or a couple of years down the road, you are able to complete the piece to your satisfaction—and delight.

- If you come up with more than one piece that you would love to read, of course feel free to write each of those pieces.

Where Do I Go From Here?

YOU CAN GO in any direction you choose. You can continue writing for your own pleasure; you can, if you like, attempt to publish some of your work; you can try to set up a public reading of your work; you can work toward becoming a professional writer; or you can put writing aside for a while (or forever) and try some other activity.

If you want to keep writing, you may continue to rely on your regular critics, or you may wish to find new ones. If you'd like to take a credit or noncredit course in writing, by all means do so: this book has prepared you very well for it. Many colleges offer degree programs, both undergraduate and graduate, in creative writing; some offer degrees in related fields, such as professional writing, editing, publishing studies, and technical writing.

You may also want to attend a writers' workshop or conference, or join a writers' center, or become a member of a writers' club or organization. None of this is necessary, but after reading this book you'll be well prepared for membership in any of these institutions.

If you'd like to proceed with guidance from other, more advanced guides to creative writing, here are some recommended volumes:

Three Genres by Stephen Minot (Prentice-Hall) is an excellent and concise guide to the writing of fiction, poetry, and plays. Its approach is highly technical—that is, it is oriented toward craft rather than inspiration. In many ways, *Three Genres* builds on what you have learned from this volume, and it is therefore an excellent next step.

Writing Down the Bones by Natalie Goldberg (Shambhala) is a highly unusual writing book that approaches writing as a process of personal and spiritual growth—which of course it is. At once inspiring and intensely practical, this book can be used as a writing guide or simply read for pleasure. Recommended for both fiction writers and poets.

On Writing Well by William Zinsser (Harper & Row) is the best and most concise guide to writing nonfiction. Writers interested in nonfiction cannot find a more useful book.

All of these books complement rather than duplicate one another, and all are excellent follow-ups to this book. None is necessary, however; if you'd like to continue writing on your own, without additional guidance from other books, that's just fine.

ADDITIONAL WRITING EXERCISES

BY NOW CHANCES are good that you're finding things to write about on your own, and you no longer need writing exercises to help you get started.

However, it never hurts—and often helps—to have some additional exercises on hand for those times when you want or need inspiration.

The twenty-five exercises you've done (or at least read) in this book so far have all been very successful for many of my creative writing students in the past. Here are some other exercises that have been successful for my students somewhat less frequently. At least a few should prove inspiring to you.

1) Write a piece in which someone or something gets filled up.

2) Write a piece that relates somehow to light and darkness.

3) Write about the strangest thing that ever happened to a) a popcorn vendor at the state fair, or b) a vacuum cleaner salesman. This incident may or may not have occurred on the job; it may be realistic, fantastic, or somewhere in between.

4) Write a funny piece in which someone opens a mailbox, and/or a completely serious piece in which someone gets hit in the face with a pie.

5) Write a piece that connects these two incidents in any manner: a man's hat blows off his head; six hours later, a child falls off a swing.

6) Write a piece that will make your reader sad, angry, or shaken up.

7) Take a newspaper story (or some element of it) and turn it into a story or poem.

8) Write a piece about a floating world.

9) Write a story for children that's not cute in any way. It may or may not be completely serious.

10) Write a story or poem that takes place in the second grade. It may or may not be based on a real experience. Write it in such a way that it is interesting to adult readers.

11) Pick four nouns. Write a piece using all four. Variations: four verbs; four adjectives. If four seems too many, try three.

12) For twenty-four hours, don't say anything at all to anyone. Carry a notebook around with you. Spend a good portion of your waking hours during this time writing, as the spirit moves you.

13) You're sitting on a Greyhound bus, waiting to pull out of the station. Somebody odd (but not necessarily offensive) gets on and sits next to you. Take it from here.

14) Write a piece in which someone oversteps a social or other boundary.

15) Outline a short story from beginning to end, using any method or combination of methods from chapter 60.

16) Write a pseudo-essay: a fake (and entertaining) inaugural address, Dear Abby column, college catalogue, annual report, high school graduation speech, petition, advertisement, press release, editorial, celebrity interview, etc. Your piece may be humorous, serious, or both.

17) Write an experimental piece.

18) Write a piece that could be entitled "The Magic _____" or "The Enchanted _____." Fill in either blank as you choose. The piece does not have to be for children, nor does it

have to have any of the elements of a fairy tale—though it can, if you want it to.

19) Do something deliberately odd in public, with other people watching. Use the results as the basis of a piece. (Important: don't do anything that could cause harm to anyone, including yourself.)

20) Begin a piece with the words "My mother is a _____," "My mother was a _____," or "I wish my mother were a _____." Fill in the blank with anything you please. You may substitute any of these words for "mother": father, son, daughter, husband, wife, grandfather, grandmother, granddaughter, grandson, boyfriend, girlfriend, fiancé, fiancée, uncle, aunt, nephew, niece, cat, dog.

21) Person A writes down a line. Person B must write a piece using Person A's line somewhere in it. As the piece develops, the line may be altered, moved, or discarded.

Scott Edelstein has taught creative writing at Oberlin College, the University of Minnesota, Metropolitan State University, and other colleges. About a hundred of his short stories and articles have appeared in magazines and anthologies, and he writes a regular column for *Writer's Digest*. A former book, newspaper, and magazine editor, he is the author of *The Indispensable Writer's Guide* and several other books about writing.